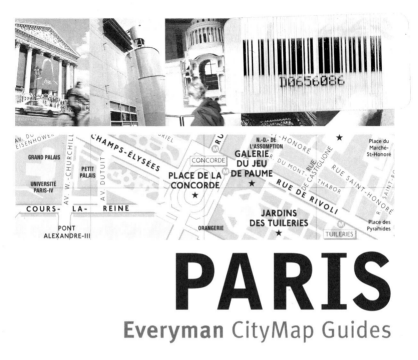

PARIS
Everyman CityMap Guides

HOW TO USE THIS GUIDE

The **Welcome to Paris!** fold-out provides valuable information, handy tips and useful addresses to help you make the most of your visit.

The area sections **A, B, C, D, E, F, G** and **H** have a double-page of addresses (restaurants - listed in ascending order of price - cafés, bars, music venues and stores) as well as a fold-out map for the relevant area with the essential places to see (indicated on the map by a star ★). These places are by no means all that Paris has to offer but to us they are unmissable.

The grid-referencing system (**A** B2) makes it easy for the reader to pinpoint addresses quickly on the map.

The **Transport and hotels in Paris** fold-out provides all the practical information you need to find your way around the city and a selection of the best hotels.

The **Thematic index** lists all the sites and addresses featured in this guide.

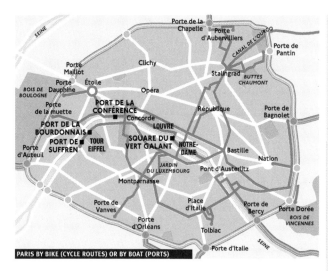

PARIS BY BIKE (CYCLE ROUTES) OR BY BOAT (PORTS)

PARIS BY BOAT

'Bateaux-mouches'
Discover the city with a
1-hour cruise. Various
companies (see map):
Vedettes de Paris
→ *Port de Suffren (7ᵗʰ)*
Tel. 01 44 18 08 03
M° Bir-Hakeim. Price: 50F
Bateaux-Parisiens
→ *Port de la Bourdonnais
(7ᵗʰ) Tel. 01 44 11 33 44*
M° Trocadéro. Price: 50F
Vedettes du Pont-Neuf
→ *1, sq. du Vert-Galant (1ˢᵗ)*
Tel. 01 46 33 98 38
M° Pont-Neuf. Price: 50F
**Compagnie des
bateaux-mouches**
→ *Port de la Conférence (7ᵗʰ)*
Tel. 01 42 25 96 10
M° Alma-Marceau. Price: 40F
Batobus
From the Eiffel Tower to the
Hôtel-de-Ville in 6 stages.
→ *Port de la Bourdonnais
(7ᵗʰ) Tel. 01 44 11 33 99*
M° Trocadéro. Per stage: 20F
Whole day: 60F

PARIS ON SKATES

It is still not clear where you
are permitted to skate in
Paris. Experienced skaters
take advantage of side-
walks, roads and cycle
tracks alike.
Pari Roller (C C2)
→ *Tel. 01 43 36 89 81*
This company organizes a
free 15-mile outing every
Friday (departs 10pm from
40, ave. d'Italie). Not for
beginners.
Nomades (C C2)
→ *37, bd Bourdon (4ᵗʰ)*
Tel. 01 44 54 07 44
Rental, classes and
courses. Free outing on
Sun (departs 2.30pm from
in front of the store).

SHOPPING

Opening times
Mon–Sat 10am–7pm
Some stores close on Mon.
Late-night opening
On Thu. in most

department stores
(Le Printemps and
La Samaritaine are open
until 10pm and Les Galeries
Lafayette until 9pm).
Sales
Twice a year: January and
July/Aug.
Department stores
BHV (C D3)
→ *52, rue de Rivoli (4ᵗʰ)*
La Samaritaine (B F4)
→ *19, rue de la Monnaie (1ˢᵗ)*
Le Bon Marché (A A2)
→ *22, rue de Sèvres (7ᵗʰ)*
Les Galeries Lafayette (EA6)
→ *40, bd Haussmann (9ᵗʰ)*
Le Printemps (E A6)
→ *64, bd Haussmann (9ᵗʰ)*

MARKETS

Flea markets (les 'puces')
Puces de Saint-Ouen
→ *M° Porte-de-Saint-Ouen
Sat–Mon 7.30am–7pm.*
The oldest and biggest of
the city's flea markets.
Quality goods spread over
a dozen markets.

CHIC PARIS

**Ave. Montaigne,
Rue François-Iᵉʳ (D** C2)
The most famous names
in *haute couture*.
**Opéra, Madeleine
(B** C2)
Luxury foodstores,
department stores.
Saint-Honoré (B C2)
The newest and best
designers.
Pl. des Victoires (B E2)
Ready-to-wear, top labels.
Pl. Vendôme (B E2)
Hôtel Ritz, the big names
in jewelry design.
Sèvres-Babylone (A A2)
Ready-to-wear, top
designers and interior
design.

TRENDY PARIS

Oberkampf (F B1)
The latest 'in' area.
Ménilmontant (G D6)
Attracts a new generation
of party animals.
Bercy, Tolbiac (H E3)
Nightlife on the
waterfront.
Le Marais (C E3)
Jewish and gay district.
Bastille (F B3)
Classic Paris nightlife.
**Butte-aux-Cailles
(H** A4)
For the village
atmosphere of
yesteryear.

IMMORTAL PARIS

Latin Quarter (A C1)
Galleries, bookstores,
literary cafés.
Champs-Élysées (D C1)
The famous triumphal
arch.
Montparnasse (A A3)
The haunt of artists and
bohemians for decades.

BY BOAT

BY BIKE

ETHNIC PARIS

**Avenue d'Ivry /
Porte de Choisy**
Little Chinatown.
**Rue and Bd de
Belleville**
Asia: on Rue de
Belleville. North Africa:
on Bd de Belleville.
Rue des Rosiers
Jewish restaurants and
patisseries.
Passage Brady
India in miniature along
this attractive covered
passageway.
Barbès
Africa and North Africa
at Château-Rouge
market: various stores
and small restaurants.

PARIS IN FIGURES

- 33½ sq miles
- 20 arrondissements
- 80 quartiers (districts)
- 2 million inhabitants
in the city center
- 21 million visitors each
year ■ the 5th largest
city in the EU ■ 8 miles
of the Seine river

THE 20 ARRONDISSEMENTS

VIEWS OF THE CITY

Eiffel Tower (D B4)
The best view of Paris.
On a clear day you can
see for 40 miles.
Samaritaine (B F4)
From the circular terrace
on the 11th floor of this
department store.
Sacré-Cœur (E C3)
From the top of the dome.
Montparnasse (A A3)
From the top of the tower.
**Institut du Monde Arabe
(H** B1) Stunning view of
the Île Saint-Louis and Île
de la Cité from the 9th-
floor terrace.
Parc de Belleville (G D6)
Great views from the park
and Rue des Envierges.

GREEN SPACES

Parks and woods
Paris has around
5,440 acres of park and
woodland covering 20%
of the city's total area.

These include two huge
woodland areas: the Bois
de Boulogne and the Bois
de Vincennes and over
400 parks and gardens.
Opening times
Mon-Fri 7.30am–9.30pm,
Sat-Sun 9am-9.30pm
(until 5.30pm in winter).
Bois de Boulogne
→ Porte Dauphine / Porte
d'Auteuil. M° Porte-Maillot
2,088 acres of woodland
containing 9 miles of cycle
tracks, 17 miles of bridlepaths and numerous
footpaths. Bicycle rental
is available at the
entrance to the Jardin
d'Acclimatation and
at the lower lake's pier.
Bois de Vincennes
→ M° Porte-Dorée /
Château-de-Vincennes
2,500 acres of woodland,
pedestrian pathways,
bridlepaths and cycle
circuits. Lakes (boating),
playgrounds and a bird-
watching observatory

(near the Dauphine round-
about).

GUIDED TOURS

**Caisse Nationale des
Monuments Historiques
(C** F4)
→ Hôtel de Sully (4th)
Tel. 01 44 61 20 00
Organized tours of places
normally closed to the
public.
History of Paris
→ 82, rue Taitbout (9th)
Tel. 01 45 26 26 77
Guided theme-tours.
Program changes every
2 months.
Paris-Story
→ 11 bis, rue Scribe (9th)
Tel. 01 42 66 62 06
Apr–Oct 9am–8pm;
Nov–Mar 9am-6pm.
40-min film depicting
2,000 years of the history
of Paris, projected onto
a panoramic screen
with a soundtrack in
13 languages.

PARIS BY BICYCLE

Paris has around 90 miles
of cycle routes (see map
above). Some of the best:
• from Bd St-Germain to
Bastille (via the islands);
• from Bastille to La
Villette (via Bd Richard-
Lenoir, Canal St-Martin
and Canal de L'Ourcq);
• from Bastille to the
Promenade Plantée
(via Ave. Daumesnil
and Bd Diderot).
Rental, bike rides
Paris à vélo,
c'est sympa (F** B3)
→ 37, bd Bourdon (4th)
Tel. 01 48 87 60 01
M° Bastille
Bicycle rental, guided tours
and organized bike rides.
**Maison Roue Libre/RATP
(C** C2)
→ 95 bis, rue Rambuteau
(1st) Tel. 01 53 46 43 77
M° Châtelet-Les-Halles
Bicycle rental.

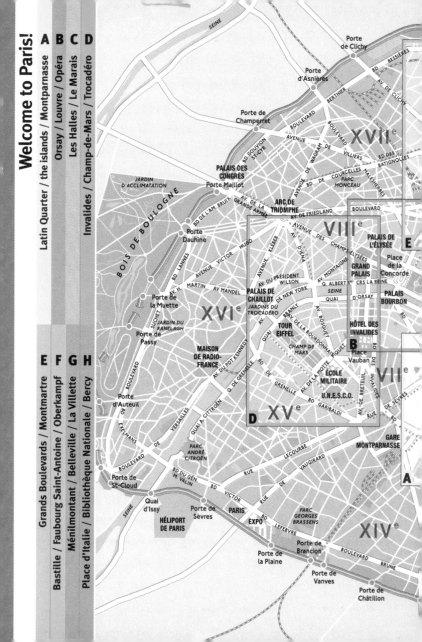

Welcome to Paris!

A Latin Quarter / the islands / Montparnasse

B Orsay / Louvre / Opéra

C Les Halles / Le Marais

D Invalides / Champ-de-Mars / Trocadéro

E Grands Boulevards / Montmartre

F Bastille / Faubourg Saint-Antoine / Oberkampf

G Ménilmontant / Belleville / La Villette

H Place d'Italie / Bibliothèque Nationale / Bercy

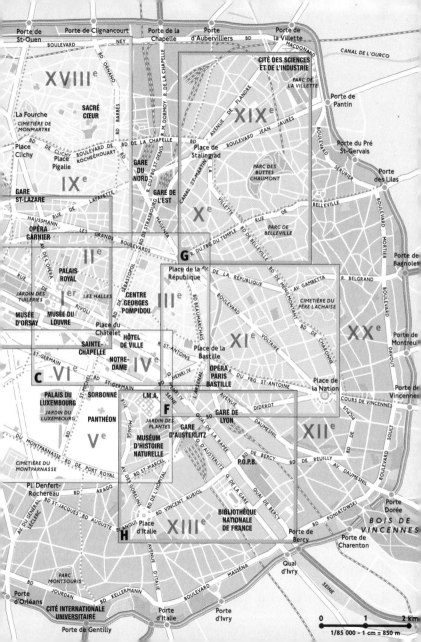

THE TOP OF LA SAMARITAINE

Allows you free entry to 70 museums/monuments in and around Paris.

CALENDAR OF EVENTS

End February/March
Banlieue Bleues (jazz festival at Seine Saint-Denis); Agricultural Show.
Mid-March
International contemporary art fair.
Early April
Paris Marathon.
End April/May
Paris fair.
End May/June
French Open Championship (tennis) at Rolland-Garros.
June
Festival of Music (21st); Cinema festival (last weekend); Gay Pride (end June)
July
Jazz festival (La Villette); Bastille Day (Firemen's Ball and firework display, 13th, military parade,

14th); the Tour de France arrives at the Champs-Élysées end of July.
July/August
Film festival (La Villette); Paris quartiers' summer festival (dance, concerts).
September
Garden Show; Heritage Open Days (properties usually closed to the public open for the day).
Mid-Sep./end-Dec.
Fall festival (dance, theater, music).
October
Grape picking in Montmartre (1st weekend).

USEFUL NUMBERS

Tourist office (D C1)
→ 127, ave. Champs-Élysées (8th) Tel. 08 36 68 31 12
Lost property
→ Tel. 01 55 76 20 20
Police
→ Tel. 17
Samu (ambulance)
→ Tel. 15

WWW.

Sites on Paris
→ paris-web.com
→ paris-touristoffice.com
→ paris-france.org
Cultural news, listings, and information
→ pariscope.com
→ fluctuat.net
→ cyberparis.com
→ cinetv.com
→ legrandrex.com
Museums
→ paris.org/Musees/
→ louvre.fr
→ musee-orsay.fr
→ cnac-gp.fr/Pompidou
Accommodation
→ france-hotel-guide.com /75paccue.htm
→ homerental.fr
Going out
Parisian bistros
→ zingueurs.com
Trendy Paris
→ novaplanet.com
Cybercafés
→ cybercaptive.com

24-HOUR PARIS

Bakeries
Boulangerie de l'Ancienne Comédie
→ 10, rue de l'Ancienne-Comédie (6th)
Tel. 01 43 26 89 72. Daily.
Chemists
Pharmacie Rico
→ 6, pl. Félix Éboué (12th)
Tel. 01 43 43 19 03. Daily.
Pharmacie Derhy
→ 84, ave. des Champs-Élysées (8th)
Tel. 01 45 62 02 41. Daily.
Restaurants
Au pied de cochon
→ 6, rue Coquillière (1st)
Tel. 01 40 13 77 00. Daily.
À la tour de Montlhéry
→ 5, rue des Prouvaires
Tel. 01 42 36 21 82 (1st)
Mon–Fri.
Tobacconists
La Favorite
→ 3, bd St-Michel (5th)
Tel. 01 43 54 08 02
Daily 7am–2am.
La Havane
→ 4, pl. de Clichy (9th)
Tel. 01 48 74 67 56
Mon–Thu 6.30am–5am,
Fri–Sun open 24 hours.

SUNDAY OPENING

Shopping
Some stores open along the Champs-Élysées (e.g. Virgin Méga Store), on the Place des Vosges and the Rue des Francs-Bourgeois.
Museums
All museums open on Sun.
Flea markets
Sat–Mon.
Skating or cycling
On Sun the banks of the Seine are closed to traffic.
→ Mar–Nov 10am–4pm.

Latin Quarter / the islands / Montparnasse

The Île de la Cité is the historic and geographic heart of Paris, filled with remnants of the old royal city. On the Rive Gauche (Left Bank) is St-Germain des-Prés with its post-war literary cafés, and the Quartier Latin with its art-house and experimental cinemas, universities and publishing houses. The Place de l'Odéon has held on to its former elegance, and the Rue St-André-des-Arts its medieval alleyways but the "Boul' Mich" (Bd St-Michel), joining onto the Luxembourg gardens, is now bereft of much of its former charm. It is worth making your way through the maze of streets around the Panthéon to the pretty Rue Mouffetard and its numerous little shops.

LA TAVERNE HENRY IV · KIOSQUE FLOTTANT

RESTAURANTS

Crêperie Josselin (A A3)
→ 67, rue du Montparnasse (14th)
Tel. 01 43 20 93 50
Tue-Fri noon–2.30pm, 6–11.30pm;
Sat-Sun noon–11pm.
No one should visit Montparnasse without stopping off to sample the famous *galettes bretonnes* (thick pancakes). Friendly atmosphere, typical Breton décor and superb crêpes. From 22F–57F per *galette*.

Taverne Henry IV (A D1)
→ 13, pl. du Pont-Neuf (1st) Tel. 01 43 54 27 90
Mon-Fri noon–8.30pm;
Sat noon–4pm. Closed Aug.
Robert Cointepas has manned the bar here for the past 40 years. More than 20 different types of wine available by the glass and delicious pork dishes from 30F.

Le Réminet (A E2)
→ 3, rue des Grands-Degrés (5th) Tel. 01 44 07 04 24
Closed Mon and Tue.
Chef Hugues Gourmay boldly marries different spices and flavors. Seasonal produce is cleverly integrated, with outstandingly delicious results. Reservations recommended in the evening. Set menu 110F, à la carte 210F.

Kiosque Flottant (A E2)
→ Port de Montebello (5th) Tel. 01 53 61 23 29
April–Sep: daily 10am–2pm
Sample a duck magret with raspberries in this splendid setting: a boat moored right at the foot of Notre-Dame.
À la carte 150F.

La Coupole (A C4)
→ 102, bd du Montparnasse (14th)
Tel. 01 43 20 14 20
Daily, continual service.
Once the meeting place of poets and writers in the 30s, today it still looks just the same, even after renovation. Art-Deco furnishings: painted pillars and chandeliers. Average cooking but good for people-watching.
Set menu 189F, 138F after 10.30pm.

Bouillon Racine (A D2)
→ 3, rue Racine (6th)
Tel. 01 44 32 15 60
Daily 7.30am–midnight.
A credit to Belgium, this stunning sea-green Art-Nouveau setting offers thirty different beers. Fish *waterzooi* (soup), knuckle of lamb *confit* and exquisite coffee *liégeois* (coffee ice cream with whipped cream) served

RUE DU ST-MICHEL

RUE AUGUSTE-COMTE

RUE NOTRE-DAME-DE

BD RA

RUE VAVIN

R. D'ASSAS

MONTPARNASSE-
BIENVENÜE

RUE DU MONTPARNASSE

BOULEVARD 3

ÉCOLE
DES MINES

LUXEMBOURG
(R.E.R.)

N.-D.-DES-CHAMPS

RUE LITTRÉ

R. DE RENNES

RUE GUYNEMER

ÉCOLE
DES MINES

LUXEMBOURG
(R.E.R.)

ST-PLACIDE

RUE DE VAUGIRARD

RUE DU CHERCHE-

RUE FERRAND

MUSÉE
HÉBERT

JARDIN
DU LUXEMBOURG

PALAIS DU
LUXEMBOURG
(SÉNAT)

FONTAINE
DE MÉDICIS

R. DE MÉDICIS

RUE DE FLEURUS

RUE MADAME

RUE DE VAUGIRARD

RUE D'ASSAS

ST-JOSEPH-
DES-CARMES

RUE DE RENNES

RENNES

RUE DE L'ABBÉ-GRÉGOIRE

SAINT-VINCENT-
DE-PAUL

ST-IGNACE

HÔPITAL
LAENNEC

RUE DE SÈVRES

2

RUE DE VAUGIRARD

VIe

THÉÂTRE DE
L'ODÉON
PL. P.-
Claudel

RUE DE TOURNON

R. DE VAUGIRARD

RUE GARANCIÈRE

RUE BONAPARTE

RUE CASSETTE

RUE

ST-SULPICE

Place
St-Sulpice

PLACIDE

ST-SULPICE

RENNES

RUE DE MÉZIÈRES

RUE DU CHERCHE-MIDI

BOULEVARD RASPAIL

SÈVRES-
BABYLONE

RUE DE SÈVRES

UNI
PA

ODÉON

Carrefour
de l'Odéon

R. ST-SULPICE de l'Odéon

R. DE L'ODÉON

RUE DE SEINE

RUE MONSIEUR

RUE
4 VENTS

RUE MABILLON

RUE DU FOUR

R. DU FOUR

RUE DES CANETTES

R. DE SÈVRES

SQUARE
DES
SAINTS-PÈRES

RUE DE GRENELLE

SQUARE
CHAISE-
RÉCAMIER

RUE DE LA CHAISE

RUE DES
MISSIONS-
ÉTRANGÈRES

RUE DU BAC

RUE DE BABYLONE

ST-
GERMAIN

BD
RASPAIL

COUR DU
ROHAN

ST-ANDRÉ

R. DAUPHINE

QUARTIER
LATIN

MABILLON

ST-GERMAIN-
DES-PRÉS

ÉGLISE
SAINT-GERMAIN-
DES-PRÉS

ST-VLADIMIR-
LE-GRAND

UNIVERSITÉ
PARIS-V

ST-THOMAS-
D'AQUIN

RUE DES SAINTS-PÈRES

RUE DU PRÉ-
AUX-CLERCS

R. DE GRENELLE

MUSÉE
DINA-VIERNY

RUE DE VARENNE

BOULEVARD SAINT-GERMAIN

VIIe

RUE DU BAC

RUE DU BAC

PLACE
DU PONT-
NEUF

C°. DE CONTI

INSTITUT
DE FRANCE

HÔTEL
DES MONNAIES

RUE GUÉNÉGAUD

RUE MAZARINE

RUE DE SEINE

RUE DES BEAUX-ARTS

ÉCOLE DES
BEAUX-ARTS

RUE BONAPARTE

R. JACOB

RUE DE L'UNIVERSITÉ

R. DE VERNEUIL

MINISTÈRE DES
TRANSPORTS

PENTEMONT

RUE DE GRENELLE

RUE DU BAC

SAINTE-CHAPELLE

PLACE DAUPHINE

MUSÉE DU MOYEN-ÂGE
PANTHÉON
JARDIN DU LUXEMBOURG

★ **Sainte-Chapelle** (**A** D1)
→ 1, quai de l'Horloge (1st)
Tel. 01 53 73 78 50
Daily 10am–5pm.
This Gothic architectural
gem was built at the
request of Saint Louis
(1245–8) to house Christ's
Crown of Thorns. The use
of abutments instead of
flying buttresses, metal
frames and iron clamps
enabled the construction
of the extraordinary
50 ft-high stained-glass
windows. They depict
some 1,134 scenes
from the Old and New
testaments along with the
story of Louis IX receiving
the holy relics.

★ **Pont-Neuf /**
Place Dauphine (**A** C1)
The oldest, longest and
most famous of Paris'
bridges was built in 1607
to allow King Henry IV to
cross from one bank to the
other. In 1985 Bulgarian
artist and sculptor Christo
completely wrapped the
bridge in fabric, turning it
into a work of art. At the far
end of the Île de la Cité is
Place Dauphine, the second
of the capital's royal squares,
built in 1607 in honor of the
Dauphin.
★ **Cathédrale**
Notre-Dame (**A** E1)
→ 1, pl. du Parvis-de-Notre-
Dame (4th) Daily 8am–6.45pm.

This impressive cathedral,
begun in 1163, represents
Gothic architecture at its
most impressive. Here agin
the use of flying buttresses
permitted windows to be
introduced on a scale that
was previously unheard of.
The strikingly beautiful
rose window to the south,
the delicacy of the flying-
buttresses and the fragility
of the spire make this a
true masterpiece of Gothic
architecture.
★ **Île Saint-Louis** (**A** F1)
This tiny island was
nothing more than pasture-
land when Christophe
Marie began building a
village here in 1614. More

intimate than its neighbo
the Île de la Cité, it is full
superb old houses, narro
streets and flights of mos
steps leading down to the
Seine.
★ **Église Saint-Germai**
des-Prés (**A** C1)
→ 3, pl. St-Germain-des-Pr
(6th) Tel. 01 43 25 41 71
Daily 8.30am–7.30pm.
The oldest church in Paris,
built in AD 990 on the
foundations of a
Merovingian basilica, it wa
uncovered in 1970. It has
12th-century ambulatory
clocktower and choir, ribb
vaulting in the 17th-centur
nave and an 18th-century
presbytery.

A

MONMARTRE

BERCY VILLAGE

LE LOUVRE

Les Puces de Montreuil
→ *M° Porte-de-Montreuil*
Sat–Mon 8am–6pm.
The most popular of the
three flea markets: second-
hand clothes and mountains
of bric-à-brac.

Les Puces de Vanves
→ *ave. Georges-Lafenestre*
M° Porte-de-Vanves
Sat–Sun 7am–7pm.
Delightful bric-à-brac and
average antiques at
reasonable prices. Go to
Rue Marc-Saignier for
second-hand clothes and
discounted kitchen utensils.

Food markets
Each quartier has its own
market (daily or 2/3 times
a week).
→ *rue Montorgueil (2nd)*
Daily.
→ *rue Mouffetard (5th)*
Tue, Thu, Sat.
→ *bd Richard-Lenoir (11th)*
Thu, Sun.
→ *rue d'Aligre (11th)*
Tue–Sun.

→ *bd de Belleville (20th)*
Tue, Fri.
Flower markets
→ *Île de la Cité*
pl. Louis-Lépine (1st)
Mon–Sat 8am–7pm.
→ *pl. de la Madeleine (8th)*
Mon–Sat 8am–7.30pm.
→ *pl. des Ternes (17th)*
Tue–Sun 8am–7pm.

SHOWS

Reservations
FNAC (**A** A3)
→ *136, rue de Rennes (6th)*
Tel. 08 36 68 04 56
Daily 24 hours.
Virgin Méga Store (**D** C1)
→ *52, ave. Champs-Élysées*
(8th) Tel. 01 49 53 50 00
Daily noon–midnight.
Reductions
FNAC
→ *Tel. 08 03 02 00 40*
Standby seats available
3 hours before
performances. Up to
40% reduction on same-
or following-day tickets.

Theater kiosk
→ *pl. de la Madeleine (8e) and
in front of Gare Montparnasse
(14th) Tue–Sat 12.30–8pm,
Sun 12.30–4pm.*
50% reduction for same-
day performances.
National theaters
Limited number of seats at
50F, every Thu (from the
individual theaters).
Independent theaters
Seats at 70F for under
26-year-olds.
**Concert, movie, theater
information**
Officiel des spectacles
→ *At newspaper kiosks,
every Wed, 2F*
Listings of shows, plays,
concerts and movies...
Pariscope
→ *At newspaper kiosks,
every Wed, 3F*
Complete listings of cultural
events throughout Paris.
Lylo
→ *FNAC, and bars
Every 3 weeks (free)*
Lists all the city's concerts.

MUSEUMS

Opening times
Usually 10am–6pm. Closed
Mon (municipal museums)
or Tue (national museums).
Children
Most museums offer
guided tours, activities and
workshops for children.
Enquire at the individual
museums.
Concessions
Generally available to
students, 18–25 year-olds,
the over-60s and the
unemployed. Varies
depending on the museum.
Musée du Louvre (**B** E3)
→ *Reduced-priced entry after
3pm every day, free on Sun.*
Free entry
National museums
→ *1st Sun. of the month*
Carte Musée Monuments
→ *Pass available from
participating museums, FNAC,
tourist offices and subway
stations. Pass for 1, 3 or 5
days (80F, 160F or 240F).*

by the jug. La Gueuze et l'Écaille bar, adjacent to the restaurant, has seafood dishes and sells an impressive range of Belgian beers. Set menu 189F.

CAFÉS, TEAROOMS

Le Flore (A B1)
➔ *172, bd St-Germain (6th)*
Tel. 01 45 48 55 26
Daily 7am–1.30am.
Once the haunt of Left-Bank heroes such as Picasso, Hemingway, Camus and Sartre, this café still attracts the city's artists, intellectuals, and writers who've just been to see their editor in a nearby publishing house. The first floor tends to be a quieter place to sit. Pricey.

Café de la Mairie (A B2)
➔ *8, pl. St-Sulpice (5th)*
Tel. 01 43 26 67 82
Mon-Sat 7am–2pm.
Opposite the church of St-Sulpice, this popular café has become the hang-out for literature lovers. The ashes of Nina Berberova were scattered just in front under the plane tree. Readings on Tue evenings except in summer. Pleasant terrace.

Charlotte de l'Île (A F2)
➔ *24, rue Saint-Louis-en-*

l'Île *(4th) Tel. 01 43 54 25 83*
Thu–Sun noon–8pm.
Tiny store with an enchanting décor where you can sample 36 blends of tea, divine hot chocolate and delicious fresh pastries.

La Viennoiserie (A C2)
➔ *8, rue de l'École-de-Médecine (6th)*
Tel. 01 43 26 60 48
Mon-Fri 9am–7pm.
Tiny patisserie-cum-tea room where a mixed crowd of regulars and students come on a daily basis for the delicious Jewish cakes, pastries, the enormous ice-cream floats and Viennese chocolates. Savory tarts and salads at lunchtime. Set menu 36F.

BARS, CINEMAS, MUSIC VENUES

La Villa (A C1)
➔ *29, rue Jacob (6th)*
Tel. 01 43 26 60 00
Mon-Sat 6pm–2am.
In the magnificent vaulted cellar of the modern hotel Villa St-Germain this has become since its opening in 1991 one of the city's leading jazz clubs. Top-quality music and performers.

Caveau de la Huchette (A D1)
➔ *5, rue de la Huchette*

(5th) Tel. 01 43 26 65 05
Daily from 9pm.
This medieval cellar-club has attracted rock 'n' roll fans for generations. Jazz and honky tonk piano at weekends.

Polly Magoo (A D2)
➔ *11, rue Saint-Jacques (5th) Tel. 01 40 29 02 18*
Daily noon–6am.
Discreet little bar with nicotine-stained posters, enticing nightowls in for a last drink.

Le Champo (A D2)
➔ *51, rue des Écoles (5th)*
Tel. 01 43 54 51 60
The most famous arthouse and independent cinema in the area.

Le P'tit Journal (A C3)
➔ *71, bd St-Michel (5th)*
Tel. 01 43 26 28 59
Mon-Sat 9am–2pm.
Atmosphere of 1950s St-Germain-des-Prés in this top-quality jazz venue with the sounds of Bolling, Zanini, Luter and Bailey.

SHOPPING

Berthillon (A F2)
➔ *31, rue St-Louis-en-l'Île (4th) Tel. 01 43 54 31 61*
Wed-Sun 10am–8pm.
Closed July-Aug.
Raspberry, mirabelle plum, honey, fig, nougat...
This world-famous

ice-cream parlor boasts some 70 different flavors.

Marché aux Fleurs (A D1)
➔ *pl. Louis-Lépine (4th)*
Daily 8am–7pm.
Flower market on the Île de la Cité: a tiny jungle right next to the Seine. Bird market on Sun.

Bouquinistes (A C1-E2)
➔ *Thu-Sun.*
Since the 19th century this leafy row of second-hand book stalls has stood on the banks of the Seine: forgotten novels, anthologies of erotica, old maps and pre-war newspapers.

Le Bon Marché (A A2)
➔ *24, rue de Sèvres (7th)*
Tel. 01 44 39 80 00
Mon-Fri 9.30am–7pm;
Thu 9.30am–9pm;
Sat 9.30am–8pm.
Has become the most chic department store, complete with beauty treatment spa and high-quality delicatessen.

Christian Tortu (A C2)
➔ *Carrefour de l'Odéon (6th) Tel. 01 43 26 02 56*
Mon-Sat 9am–8pm;
Sun 11am–7pm.
The shop window of this 'artist' (you wouldn't dare call him a florist) gives you some idea of what the Garden of Eden must have been like.

NOTRE-DAME

ÎLE SAINT-LOUIS

SAINT-GERMAIN-DES-PRÉS

NEUF
UPHINE
QUAI DE L'HORLOGE
D
ÎLE
DE
LA
CITÉ
CHÂTELET
QUAI DE GESVRES
E
RUE DE LA VERRERIE
RUE DE RIVOLI
F

SAINTE-
CHAPELLE
QUAI DE LA CORSE
Place
L.-Lépine
HÔTEL
DE VILLE
HÔTEL-
DE-VILLE
LE MARAIS

PALAIS DE
JUSTICE
BD DU PALAIS
RUE DE LA CITÉ
CITÉ
HÔTEL-DIEU
QUAI DE L'HÔTEL-DE-VILLE
ST-GERVAIS-
ST-PROTAIS
ST-PAUL

AI DES ORFÈVRES
PRÉFECTURE
DE POLICE
Pl. du Parvis-
Notre-Dame
QUAI D'ARCOLE
QUAI AUX FLEURS
IVe
RUE
R.-G.-L'ASNIER
RUE
CHARLEMAGNE

USTINS Pl.
St-Michel
ST-MICHEL
QUAI
CATHÉDRALE
NOTRE-DAME
PONT
LOUIS-
PHILIPPE
PONT-
MARIE
HÔTEL DE
SENS

ST-MICHEL
(R.E.R.)
RUE DE
LA HUCHETTE
R. ST-JULIEN-
LE-PAUVRE
PONT ST-
LOUIS
ÎLE SAINT-LOUIS
QUAI DES
CÉLESTINS

TÉ
ST-MICHEL
SQUARE
JEAN-XXIII
PONT DE
L'ARCHEVÊCHÉ
R. ST-LOUIS-DES-DEUX-PONTS
PONT
MARIE

SAINT-SÉVERIN
CLUNY-
LA SORBONNE
ST-JULIEN-
LE-PAUVRE
QUAI MONTEBELLO
QUAI D'ORLÉANS
QUAI D'ANJOU

HERMES DE CLUNY
MUSÉE
DU MOYEN-ÂGE
RUE DES
GRANDS-DEGRÉS
Place
Maubert
QUAI DE LA TOURNELLE
ST-LOUIS-
EN-L'ÎLE
QUAI DE BÉTHUNE
ES
RUE DES
ÉCOLES
R. F. SAUTON
R. DES BERNARDINS
PT DE LA
TOURNELLE
BD HENRI-IV

SORBONNE
COLLÈGE
DE FRANCE
MAUBERT-
MUTUALITÉ
BD SAINT-GERMAIN
INSTITUT
DU MONDE
ARABE
PONT DE
SULLY

Pl. de la
Sorbonne
SAINT-JACQUES
ÉCOLES
R. DE LA MONTAGNE-
SAINTE-GENEVIÈVE
R. DES
MONGE
ST-NICOLAS-DU-
CHARDONNET
RUE DE PONTOISE
RUE DES
FOSSÉS-ST-BERNARD
Q. ST-BERNARD

CUJAS
RUE CUJAS
R. VALETTE
R.
DES
ÉCOLES
LEMOINE
UNIVERSITÉS
PARIS-VI-VII
PIERRE-ET-
MARIE-CURIE

SOUFFLOT
PANTHÉON
RUE CUJAS
SQUARE
PAUL
LANGEVIN
ST-ÉTIENNE
DU MONT
CARDINAL
LEMOINE
RUE DU CARDINAL-
RUE

QUES
Pl. du
Panthéon
RUE CLOVIS
JARDIN
CARRÉ
Place
Jussieu
JUSSIEU
RUE CUVIER

INT-JACQUES
R. P. ET
M. CURIE
R. DE L'ESTRAPADE
DESCARTES
RUE ROLLIN
Place de la
Contrescarpe
ARÈNES DE
LUTÈCE
PLACE MONGE
R. MONGE
RUE LINNÉ
JUSSIEU
RUE CUVIER
JARDIN
DES
PLANT

INSTITUT
CURIE
Ve
RUE LAG

FONDATION CARTIER

CIMETIÈRE DU MONTPARNASSE

Thermes de Cluny / Musée National du Moyen Âge (**A** D2)

…, pl. Paul-Painlevé (5ᵗʰ)
…, 01 53 73 78 00
…-Mon 9.15am–5.45pm.

…nt next to the remains of …Gallo-Roman baths …d–3rd century) stands … Hôtel des Abbés de …ny (1485–1510), the …st beautiful example of …dieval Parisian non-…gious architecture. Since …5 this has housed the …onal Museum of the …dle Ages which contains …ies, heads of kings from …e-Dame gold-work and …ics. The main attraction …e famous tapestry *La*

Dame à la Licorne (The Lady and the Unicorn).

★ **Panthéon** (**A** D3)
→ pl. du Panthéon (5ᵗʰ)
Tel. 01 44 32 18 00
Daily 10am–6.15pm.
This church, built by Louis XV, was not completed until 1789. Three years later the Assembly dedicated it to the memory of the great names of the Revolution: Mirabeau, Voltaire and Rousseau. Its status as a mausoleum was not made official until 1885, in time to accept the ashes of Victor Hugo.

★ **Jardin du Luxembourg** (**A** C3)
→ pl. Edmond-Rostand (6ᵗʰ)

Daily 8am–9.45pm (5.15pm in winter).
The avenues of chestnut trees, punctuated by an astonishing series of sculptures, and the English garden and orchard with 710 varieties of apple trees make this the city's most romantic park. For over 100 years the central ornamental lake, designed by Le Nôtre (17th century), has provided a favorite sailing ground for model-boat enthusiasts.

★ **Fondation Cartier** (**A** B4)
→ 261, bd Raspail (14ᵗʰ)
Tel. 01 42 18 56 51
Daily noon–8pm.

This incredible construction of glass and steel, designed by Jean Nouvel in 1994, houses more than 900 contemporary works of art by 250 artists from all over the world.

★ **Cimetière du Montparnasse** (**A** A4)
→ 3, bd Edgar-Quinet (14ᵗʰ)
Tel. 01 44 10 86 50
Mon-Sun 9am–6pm
(5.30pm in winter).
A tribute to the writers and artists who contributed to this quartier's renown in the 19th and 20th centuries: Baudelaire, Sartre, Beauvoir, Maupassant, Dreyfus, Brancusi and more recently, Serge Gainsbourg.

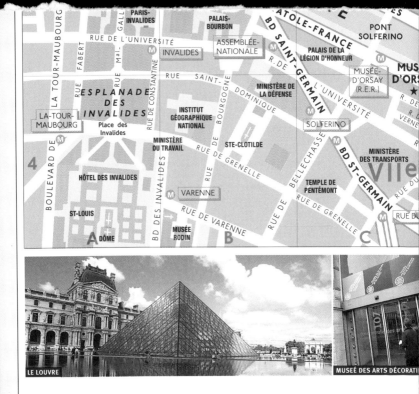

LE LOUVRE

MUSÉE DES ARTS DÉCORATI

★ Église de la Madeleine (B C2)

→ pl. de la Madeleine (8th)
Tel. 01 44 51 69 00
Mon-Sat 7.30am–1.30pm,
3.30–7pm.
Constant d'Ivry,
commissioned by
Napoleon I to build a
monument to the glory
of the French armies, came
up with a design based
on a Greek temple, similar
to that of the National
Assembly. Completed in
1842, the building, with
neither clocktower nor
cross on the exterior of
the building, is now
nevertheless used for
religous worship.

★ Place Vendôme (B D2)

Superb and austere at
the same time, this square,
inaugurated in 1699 and
built in the shape of a
rectangle with its corners
cut off, was originally a
virtually enclosed space
measuring 160 by 150 yds.
Behind the uniform 80-ft
high walls are hidden
magnificent townhouses,
one of which is the Hôtel
Ritz at n° 15.

★ Place de la Concorde (B B3)

This busy major crossroads
is, surprisingly, one of the
most beautiful spots in
Paris. It was designed for
Louis XV in 1748. Contrary

to other royal squares
it is only walled on one
side in order to maintain
the perspective of the
triumphal axis: to the east
are the Tuileries and the
Louvre palace; to the west,
the Champs-Élysées. The
Luxor obelisk, presented
by the viceroy of Egypt,
was erected in the center
of the square in 1836.

★ Galerie du Jeu de Paume (B C2)

→ pl. de la Concorde (1st)
Tel. 01 47 03 12 50
Tue noon–9.30pm;
Wed-Fri noon–7pm;
Sat-Sun 10am–7pm.
The Jeu de Paume, built
under Napoleon III, has

been used for art
exhibitions since the
early 1900s. Magnificently
restored, it re-opened in
1991 and now mounts
temporary exhibitions of
contemporary art. Next
door the Orangerie (close
until 2002) houses Mone
famous cycle of paintings
Les Nymphéas.

★ Jardins des Tuileries (B C3)

→ pl. du Carrousel (1st)
Daily 7.30am–9pm
(until 11.45pm July–Aug
and 7.30pm in winter).
In 1666, André Le Nôtre
transformed the gardens
the Château des Tuileries
into a French-style garden

B

PLACE DE LA CONCORDE

PLACE VENDÔME

LA MADELEINE

The proximity of the Louvre Museum has made this district a firm favorite with tourists, giving the souvenir stores the chance to invade the arcades along the Rue de Rivoli. Nevertheless, the area has lost none of its grandeur. La Madeleine boasts a number of designer tableware stores and luxurious delis; top stylists' outlets and fashion designers line Rue Saint-Honoré and the arcades of Place Vendôme shelter the Ritz Hotel and the most famous jewelry stores. To escape the uproar of the streets head for the peaceful gardens of the Palais-Royal or the Tuileries.

IL CORTILE   L'ENTRACTE

RESTAURANTS

Café Véry (**B** C3)
→ *Jardins des Tuileries (1st)*
Tel. 01 47 03 94 84
Daily noon–midnight.
A great place to enjoy the tranquility of the Tuileries gardens and sample a dish of chicken with morels or almond and cinnamon. Allow 70F for a full meal.

Il Cortile (**B** C2)
→ *37, rue Cambon (1st)*
Tel. 01 44 58 45 67
Mon-Fri noon–2.30pm,
7.30–10.30pm.
One of the best Italian restaurants in Paris, created by Alain Ducasse. Seasonal specialties: cuttlefish-ink cannelloni, risotto with asparagus, white Piedmont truffles... Lovely patio which is open in summer.
À la carte 300F.

Higuma (**B** E2)
→ *32 bis, rue St-Anne (1st)*
Tel. 01 47 03 38 59
Daily 11.30am–10pm.
Formica tables, cooks positioned in front of smoking woks ... *ramen* (flat noodles) and other Japanese specialties are served in this huge restaurant which attracts a clientele ranging from business people in a hurry to young *manga*-magazine readers. Set menus 35F, 63F and 70F.

Le Rouge Vif (**B** C4)
→ *48, rue de Verneuil (7th)*
Tel. 01 42 86 81 87
Mon-Fri noon–2.15pm,
8–10.45pm; Sat 8–10.45pm.
Excellent food bought fresh from the markets, obliging service, a cozy place. Set lunch menu 95F, dinner 180F–220F.

Le Grand Véfour (**B** E2)
→ *17, rue de Beaujolais (1st)*
Tel. 01 42 96 56 27
Mon-Fri 12.30–2.15pm,
7.30–10.15pm.
One of the oldest and most beautiful restaurants in Paris, situated under the arcades of the Palais-Royal. Fabulous, listed interior decor; comfortable, plush banquettes. Guy Martin, from Savoy, creates simple dishes which make the most of the quality of his produce. Remarkable wine list. Reservation advised. Set lunch menu 350F. À la carte 700F.

TEAROOMS

Angelina (**B** C3)
→ *226, rue de Rivoli (1st)*
Tel. 01 42 60 82 00
Daily 9am–7pm.
Opened in 1903 under the arcades in Rue de Rivoli,

FLANN O' BRIEN'S COLETTE DIDIER LUDOT

this English tearoom serves some of the best hot chocolate in Paris (36F), along with excellent desserts. Chocolates and pastries to go.

CAFÉS, BARS, MUSIC VENUES

Café Marly (B E3)
→ Palais du Louvre
93, rue de Rivoli (1st)
Tel. 01 49 26 06 60
Daily 8am–2pm.
An exceptional setting to stop for a drink and view I.M. Pei's pyramid and the French sculpture rooms of the Louvre museum. Pleasant service. Coffee 19F, draught beer 32F, lunch menu 250F.

L'Entracte (B E3)
→ 47, rue de Montpensier
(1st) Tel. 01 42 97 57 76
Mon–Fri 10am–2am;
Sat–Sun noon–2am.
This café has been around for centuries. Actors and audience alike from the Comédie-Française and the Théâtre du Palais-Royal come here for pre- or post-show drinks. Fresh, homemade food. Coffee 12F, draught beer 18F after 7.30pm.

Flann O' Brien's (B F3)
→ 6, rue Bailleul (1st)
Tel. 01 42 60 13 58
Daily 4pm–2am.

Excellent Irish pub serving the smoothest Guinness in town (a pint: 39F). Darts board upstairs and excellent live music most nights.

Opéra Garnier (B D1)
→ Palais Garnier
8, rue Scribe (8th)
Tel. 01 47 42 07 02
Impressive neo-Renaissance and Baroque building dating from 1858. The auditorium ceiling was repainted by Chagall in 1964. Ballet, dance and opera performances. The library, museum, Grand Staircase and Foyer are open to the public.

SHOPPING

Samaritaine (B F4)
→ 19, rue de la Monnaie
(1st) Tel. 01 40 41 20 20
Mon–Sat 9.30am–7pm
(until 10pm Thu).
Department store situated right next to the Seine. You can buy anything you could possibly need here. Magnificent view of Paris from the roof-terrace.

Anna Joliet (B E2)
→ 9, rue de Beaujolais (1st)
Tel. 01 49 27 98 60
Mon–Sat 10am–7pm.
Music boxes that will take you back to your childhood. Over 60 different

tunes can be heard escaping from this little store hidden away beneath the arcades of the Palais-Royal. Expect to pay around 200F.

Sennelier (B D4)
→ 3, quai Voltaire (7th)
Tel. 01 42 60 72 15
Mon 2–7.30pm;
Tue–Sat 9.30am–2pm.
Walking into this three-story store is like opening an old paint box. Since 1887 Sennelier has supplied artists with papers, paints, pastels or lapis lazuli in powder form (at 2,000F for 10 gms) ... all with the Sennelier stamp.

Fauchon (B C2)
→ 24, pl. de la Madeleine
(8th) Tel. 01 47 42 60 11
Mon–Sat 9.30am–7pm
(tearoom 8am–7pm).
The most famous delicatessen in Paris: preserves, pastries, cold meats, wine, tea. An incredible range of fine and expensive goods.

Shiseido (B E3)
→ 142, galerie de Valois
(1st) Tel. 01 49 27 09 09
Mon–Sat 10am–7pm.
Under the arcades of the Palais-Royal, a treasure trove of exotic perfumes created by Serge Lutens for Shiseido. Some scents on sale here are exclusive to this store.

Colette (B D3)
→ 213, rue Saint-Honoré
(1st) Tel. 01 55 35 33 90
Mon–Sat 10.30am–7.30pm.
If it is tomorrow's fashion in clothes, art, cosmetics, jewelry, etc... Colette will have it before anybody else, and sell it ... at a price. There is a mineral water bar – the most exclusive of course – a dining room in the basement and a designers' exhibition on the 1st floor. Worth a visit, just for fun.

Didier Ludot (B E3)
→ 24, galerie Montpensier
(1st) Tel. 01 42 96 06 56
Mon–Sat 10.30am–7pm.
Second-hand clothes, footwear, bags and cases whether by Chanel, Hermès, Balenciaga, Courrèges... Didier Ludot is a genuine collector of the best designs by the biggest names.

Le Louvre des Antiquaires (B E3)
→ 2, pl. du Palais-Royal
(1st) Tel. 01 42 97 27 00
Tue–Sun 11am–7pm.
Closed Aug.
Two hundred and fifty antiques dealers under the roof of a former department store. Spread over three floors are Louis XV furniture, china, gold, jewelry ...

JARDINS DES TUILERIES

...ERIE DU JEU DE PAUME

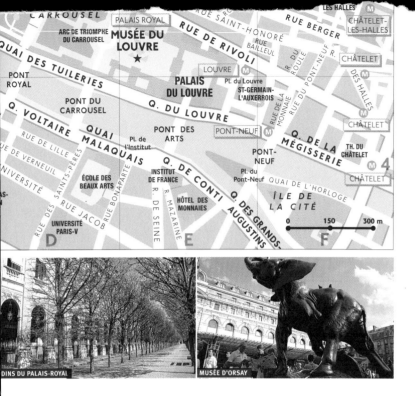

JARDINS DU PALAIS-ROYAL

MUSÉE D'ORSAY

d opened up the view to e west with a road which n became the Champs-sées. The octagonal e, the terraces running ng the Seine and the e de Rivoli, the merous chestnut and e trees growing on her side of the central enue all convey the nance of times past.

Musée du Louvre (B E3)
cour Napoléon (1st)
01 40 20 50 50
n & Wed 9am–9.30pm, -Sun 9am–5.30pm.
e largest museum in world. The Louvre's lections stretch from ancient civilizations of the Mediterranean basin to the first half of the 19th century, today completed by a new section on primitive arts. Over 800 years of French history are contained within these walls. The Cour Carrée, first begun under François I, is one of the best examples of Renaissance architecture. In 1989 Ieoh Ming Pei came up with a daring design for the Napoleon courtyard, erecting a glass pyramid at its center.

★ **Musée des Arts Décoratifs** (B D3)
→ Palais du Louvre
116, rue de Rivoli (1st)
Tel. 01 44 55 57 50
Daily 11am–6pm.
Unique collection of furniture, painting and *objets d'art* dating from the Middle Ages to the present day. Entrance tickets also give access to the Fashion and Textile and Advertising museums.

★ **Palais-Royal** (B E3)
→ pl. du Palais-Royal (2nd)
The peaceful atmosphere of the gardens and the adjacent galleries is deceptive. It was under these arcades that Parisian commerce spread in 1780, as did gambling and prostitution, while in the clubs ideas of a revolution were beginning to circulate. Home of Cardinal Richelieu, then of the Orléans family, the palace now houses the Council of State and the Ministry of Culture, whose windows overlook the main courtyard, redesigned by Buren in 1986.

★ **Musée d'Orsay** (B C4)
→ 1, rue de Bellechasse (7th)
Tel. 01 40 49 48 14
Tue-Sun 10am–5.30pm
(Thu 10am–9.45pm).
The conversion of this former railway station into a museum began in 1977. Opened in 1986, it has an unbeatable collection of art spanning the second half of the 19th century.

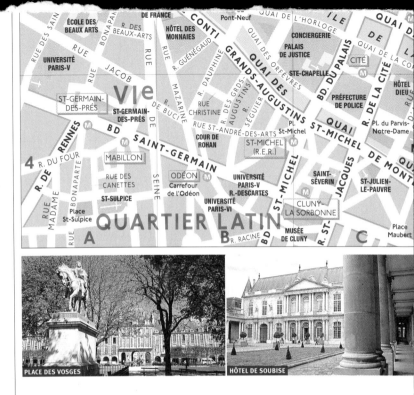

Map labels (Quartier Latin area):

DE FRANCE · Pont-Neuf · QUAI DE L'HORLOGE · ÎLE · QUAI DE
ÉCOLE DES BEAUX ARTS · R. DES BEAUX-ARTS · HÔTEL DES MONNAIES · CONTI · CONCIERGERIE · DE LA
R. GUÉNÉGAUD · QUAI DES ORFÈVRES · PALAIS DE JUSTICE · QUAI DE LA CO
UNIVERSITÉ PARIS-V · RUE JACOB · R. DAUPHINE · GRANDS-AUGUSTINS · STE-CHAPELLE · CITÉ · BD. DU PALAIS · QUAI DE LA CITÉ · HÔTEL DIEU
St-GERMAIN-DES-PRÉS · DE BUCI · RUE MAZARINE · RUE CHRISTINE · QUAI DES GDS.-AUGUSTINS · SÉGUIER · PRÉFECTURE DE POLICE · QUAI · ST-MICHEL · R. Pl. du Parvis-Notre-Dame
ST-GERMAIN-DES-PRÉS · RUE ST-ANDRÉ-DES-ARTS · St-Michel · DE LA CITÉ
BD RENNES · SAINT-GERMAIN · COUR DE ROHAN · Pl. St-Michel · ST-MICHEL (R.E.R.) · DE MONT
R. DU FOUR · MABILLON · RUE DES CANETTES · ODÉON · Carrefour de l'Odéon · UNIVERSITÉ PARIS-V R.-DESCARTES · SAINT-SÉVERIN · ST-JULIEN-LE-PAUVRE
ST-SULPICE · UNIVERSITÉ PARIS-VI · CLUNY-LA SORBONNE
Place St-Sulpice · SEINE · QUARTIER LATIN · R. RACINE · BD ST-MICHEL · MUSÉE DE CLUNY · R. ST-JACQUES · Place Maubert

PLACE DES VOSGES

HÔTEL DE SOUBISE

★ Les Halles / Montorgueil (C C2)
→ *Rue Berger (1st) / R ue Montorgueil (1st)*
With its busy market, the Rue Montorgueil, recently pedestrianized, is perhaps the last vestige of the old Halles. Always lively.

★ Centre Georges-Pompidou (C D3)
→ *Rue Saint-Martin (4th)*
Tel. 01 44 78 12 33
Mon, Wed-Sun. 11am–9pm (museum); noon–10pm (Bpi)
Opened in 1977 this very controversial avant-garde building was a joint venture between architects Renzo Piano and Richard Rogers, in response to Pompidou's (the then president's) wish to establish a multi-discipline cultural center in Paris which would be both a museum and an art center. The Musée National d'Art Moderne and the Center de Création Industrielle are both based here along with a public information library, movie theater and regular children's workshops. The layout was entirely reorganized in 1999 by Renzo Piano and Jean-François Beaudin. Panoramic views of Paris from the restaurant.

★ Hôtel-de-Ville (C D3)
→ *Pl. de l'Hôtel-de-Ville (4th)*
Until 1778 the Place de l'Hôtel-de-Ville was named Place de Grève (shore) because of its location on the river banks of the Seine. In 1357 it became the seat of municipal power. The site later became a platform for riots and demonstrations ('grève' also means 'strike') and, until 1830, public executions. The interior of the building, refurbished in the late 19th-century, contains an abundance of gilt, wood-paneling and Baccarat chandeliers, the spoils of the 3rd Republic. Each winter the area in front of the town hall is turned into a free public skating rink.

★ Hôtel de Sens (C E4)
→ *1, rue du Figuier (4th)*
Tel. 01 42 78 14 60
Closed Sun.
This 15th-century building still has corbeled turrets, a Gothic porch and a cobbled courtyard where Queen Margot once unhitched her carriage. Today it houses the Forney Library of Decorative Arts.

★ Hôtel de Sully (C F4)
→ *62, rue St-Antoine (4th)*
Tel. 01 44 61 20 00. Daily.
Dating from the 17th-century this is one of the most beautiful and impressive townhouses i

C

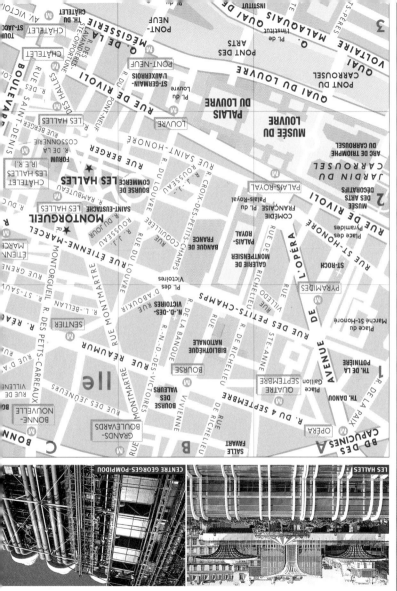

CENTRE GEORGES-POMPIDOU

LES HALLES

Map labels

TOUR ST-JACQUES
AV VICTORIA
TH. DU CHÂTELET
CHÂTELET
BOULEVARD SAINT-DENIS
R. DES LAVANDIÈRES-STE-OPPORTUNE
Q. DE LA MÉGISSERIE
PONT-NEUF
ST-JACQ
INSTITUT
PONT DES ARTS
Pl. de L'Institut
QUAI VOLTAIRE
QUAI MALAQUAIS

CHÂTELET
LES HALLES (R.E.R.)
R. DE LA COSSONNERIE
FORUM
RUE DES HALLES
ST-GERMAIN-L'AUXERROIS
R. DU PONT-NEUF
PONT-NEUF
QUAI DU LOUVRE
QUAI DU CARROUSEL
PONT DU CARROUSEL

LES HALLES
BOURSE DE COMMERCE
RUE BERGER
RUE BERGER
Pl. du Louvre
LOUVRE
PALAIS DU LOUVRE
MUSÉE DU LOUVRE

SAINT-EUSTACHE
R. RAMBUTEAU
RUE DU LOUVRE
RUE SAINT-HONORÉ
ARC DE TRIOMPHE DU CARROUSEL
JARDIN DU CARROUSEL

MONTORGUEIL
R. DU JOUR
R. J.-J. ROUSSEAU
R. COQUILLIÈRE
R. CROIX-DES-PETITS-CHAMPS
PALAIS-ROYAL
COMÉDIE FRANÇAISE
Pl. du Palais-Royal
MUSÉE DES ARTS DÉCORATIFS

R. DUC
ÉTIENNE MARCEL
RUE GRENÉ
RUE ÉTIENNE-MARCEL
RUE MONTORGUEIL
RUE MONTMARTRE
BANQUE DE FRANCE
GALERIE DE MONTPENSIER
PALAIS-ROYAL
RUE DE RICHELIEU
ST-ROCH
Place des Pyramides
RUE DE L'OPÉRA
RUE ST-HONORÉ
RUE DE RIVOLI

R. ST-SAUV
R. RÉAUMUR
RUE DES PETITS-CARREAUX
SENTIER
RUE D'ABOUKIR
Pl. des Victoires
R. N.-D.-DES-VICTOIRES
R. DE LA BANQUE
RUE DE RICHELIEU
RUE STE-ANNE
PYRAMIDES
Place du Marché St-Honoré
AVENUE DE L'OPÉRA

Île
RUE DE LA BANQUE
BIBLIOTHÈQUE NATIONALE
RUE VIVIENNE
RUE DES PETITS-CHAMPS
R. DE RICHELIEU
RUE STE-ANNE
QUATRE SEPTEMBRE
Place Gaillon
TH. DE LA POTINIÈRE

RUE DE VILLENE
RUE DES JEÛNEURS
RUE MONTMARTRE
BOURSE
BOURSE DES VALEURS
R. DU 4 SEPTEMBRE
RUE DANOU
R. DE LA PAIX

BONNE-NOUVELLE
BO
GRANDS-BOULEVARDS
RUE VIVIENNE
RUE DE RICHELIEU
SALLE FAVART
OPÉRA
BD DES CAPUCINES
A
B
C

1
2
3

The area around the Halles has been the focus of major building projects since the 1960s and makes up the heart of modern Paris. The Baltard houses, the churches of St-Eustache and of Beaubourg (the village) have all gone. The largest pedestrianized area in Europe stretches between Rue Montorgueil and the gates of St-Martin and St-Denis. Pop into the Georges-Pompidou center or explore the old quartier of Le Marais, a listed area since 1962. Here the 17th-century townhouses and narrow winding streets contain a mixture of Jewish stores, quirky, trendy boutiques, antique dealers and gay bars.

TRUMILOU   L'ESCARGOT DE MONTORGUEIL

RESTAURANTS

Minh Chau (C D3)
→ 10, rue de la Verrerie (4th) Tel. 01 42 71 13 30 Daily 9am–midnight.
Tiny Vietnamese restaurant where you can drop in for a quick bite to eat: peppered pork or shrimp curry (20–25F) accompanied by a cup of tea (3F). Very friendly.

Chez Marianne (C E3)
→ 2, rue des Hospitalières-Saint-Gervais (4th) Tel. 01 42 72 18 86 Daily.
Charming delicatessen where you can sample Jewish and Eastern European fare. An abundance of meze: falafel, kefta, tabouleh, stuffed vine leaves... You can also take out. Good choice for vegetarians. Book in advance. À la carte 55–75F.

Jo Goldenberg (C E3)
→ 7, rue des Rosiers (4th) Tel. 01 48 87 20 16 Daily 9am–midnight.
A shrine to Ashkenazi cooking: borscht, stuffed carp, chopped liver and onions, chicken soup. Inviting atmosphere and music. Daily special 80F.

Trumilou (C B2)
→ 84, quai de l'Hôtel-de-Ville (4th) Tel. 01 42 77 63 98 Daily noon–3pm, 7–11pm.

Small dishes to suit all budgets. Traditional and simple cuisine, just like home-cooking. Set menus 80F, 98F.

Chez Omar (C E2)
→ 47, rue de Bretagne (3rd) Tel. 01 42 72 36 26 Closed Sun lunch.
Traditional brasserie and the best couscous in Paris, cooked by Omar himself. À la carte 120F.

La Mule du Pape (C F3)
→ 8, rue du Pas de la Mule (3rd) Tel. 01 42 74 55 80 Mon-Fri 11am–6pm, 7–11pm Sat 11am–11pm; Sun 11am–7pm.
A few yards away from the Place des Vosges, this is a small, homely, cozy restaurant. Provençale specialties; home-made desserts. Salad with foie gras and one glass of wine 100F. À la carte 150F. Wines by the glass. It is advisable to book.

L'Escargot de Montorgueil (C C2)
→ 38, rue Montorgueil (1st) Tel. 01 42 36 83 51 Daily noon–3pm, 7–11pm.
An excellent place to taste delicious Burgundy snails in an 1870s setting.

TEAROOMS

L'Ébouillanté (C D3)
→ 6, rue des Barres (4th)

OUILLANTÉ   LE LATINA   VILLAGE SAINT-PAUL

Tel. 01 42 71 09 69
Tue-Sun noon–10pm (9pm in winter).
In a pedestrianized street opposite the church of St-Gervais-St-Protais. Mellow jazz is played in the book-lined interior, decorated in blue. The terrace is perfect for afternoon tea. Set menu 75F.

Marais Plus (C E3)
→ *20, rue des Francs-Bourgeois (3rd)*
Tel. 01 48 87 01 40
Daily 10am–7.30pm.
Store and tearoom selling fascinating and unusual toys, large and small. Exquisite savory and sweet tarts (eat in or take out).

Le Loir dans la Théière (C E3)
→ *3, rue des Rosiers (6th)*
Tel. 01 42 72 90 61
Mon-Fri 11.30am–7pm;
Sat-Sun 10am–7pm.
Sink into the comfortable old leather armchairs and enjoy a salad or delicious pastry. Excellent service. Savory tarts 48F, salads 45F.

CAFÉS, BARS, THEATERS, MUSIC VENUES

Web Bar (C E2)
→ *32, rue de Picardie (3rd)*
Tel. 01 42 72 66 55

Daily 11.30am–2am.
A heaven for cyberfans, this old silversmith work shop, converted into an Internet café, has plenty more to offer: poetry nights, debates, chess, concerts, art exhibitions...

Café Beaubourg (C D3)
→ *43, rue St-Merri (4th)*
Tel. 01 48 87 63 96
Daily 8am–1am.
Opposite the Pompidou center, this is the most chic café in the area, with an extraordinary design by architect Christian de Portzamparc.
À la carte 175F.

Duc des Lombards (C C3)
→ *42, rue des Lombards (1st) Tel. 01 42 33 22 88*
Tue-Sat from 9pm;
Sun-Mon: times vary depending on the program.
The poster-covered walls trace the history of jazz. Innovative line-up with a bias toward modern European jazz. Entrance 100F; drinks 28F.

Le Petit Opportun (C C3)
→ *15, rue des Lavandières-Sainte-Opportune (1st)*
Tel. 01 42 36 01 36
Tue–Sat from 10.30pm.
Small club that welcomes musicians from the French jazz scene, both newcomers and old timers alike: swing,

bebop, New Orleans jazz. Entrance 50–80F.

Café de la Gare (C D3)
→ *41, rue du Temple (4th)*
Tel. 01 42 78 52 51
Daily 8pm and 10pm.
The nicest of the *café-théâtres*, this venue has hosted comics, popular theater and children's shows (at 3pm) for 30 years. Entrance 100F.

Le Latina (C D3)
→ *20, rue du Temple (4th)*
Tel. 01 42 78 47 86
Since 1913 Le Latina has screened the best of Italian, Spanish, Portuguese and Latin-American films. On the first floor is a bar and dance floor complete with strutting tango dancers.

Amnesia (C E3)
→ *42, rue Vieille-du-Temple (4th) Tel. 01 42 72 16 94*
Daily 9.30am–2am.
Ivy-fronted gay bar. A colorful clientele and 1980s music in the basement. Salad and daily specials 45F.

SHOPPING

Forum des Halles (C C2)
→ *Rues Berger and Rambuteau (1st) Mon–Sat.*
Several hundred stores (one of which is FNAC), movie theater and swimming pool.

Mariage Frères (C D3)
→ *30, rue du Bourg-Tibourg (4th) Tel. 01 42 72 28 11*
Daily 10.30am–7.30pm (store), noon–7pm (rest).
Magnificent colonial-style store packed with huge round pots containing 350 varieties of tea from all over the world. Sample in house or take out. Brunch on Sun from noon–6.30pm.
À la carte 80–150F.

BHV (C D3)
→ *52, rue de Rivoli (4th)*
Tel. 01 42 77 44 79
Mon–Sat 9.30am–7pm
The place for DIY enthusiasts. The Bazar de l'Hôtel-de-Ville, right in the heart of Paris, also sells high fashion, toys perfume, books and electric appliances.

Village Saint-Paul (C E4)
→ *Rues Charlemagne and Saint-Paul (4th) Thu-Mon.*
An entire colony of little antique stores situated between Rue Saint-Paul and Rue Charlemagne along quiet passageways and courtyards.

Finkelstajn (C E3)
→ *27, rue des Rosiers (4th)*
Tel. 01 42 72 78 91
Wed-Mon 10am–7pm.
The best Jewish deli in Paris: Russian and central European specialties.

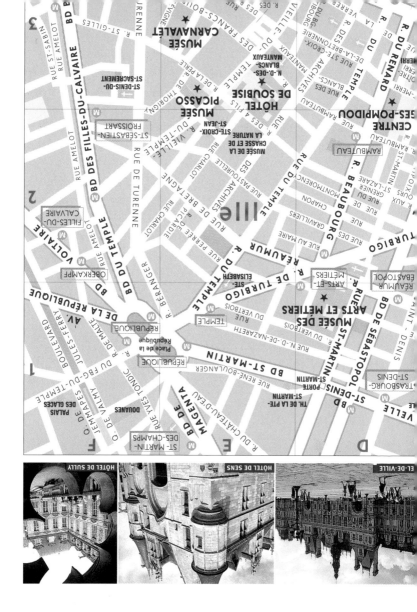

From La Concorde, the Champs-Élysées is an unforgettable sight. The famous throughfare stretches majestically to the Arc de Triomphe. Restaurants, cafés, chic night-clubs and even expensive car show-rooms draw a colorful crowd day and night. Avenue Montaigne, the epitome of luxury and home to Chanel, Christian Dior, Louis Vuitton, Nina Ricci and Christian Lacroix, the best couturiers and designers, descends toward the Seine. Les Invalides and the Champ-de-Mars stretch along the opposite bank, lined with lovely townhouses and offering impressive views of the Eiffel Tower.

RESTAURANTS

Apollon (D C3)
→ 24, rue Jean-Nicot (7th)
Tel. 01 45 55 68 47
Last orders 11pm; closed Sun.
A tiny restaurant full of Mediterranean color. Cheese from Cyprus, basil, feta and tomato salads, *souvlakis* (kebabs), ground-rice cake with lemon zest. Lunch menu 85F.

L'Ami-Jean (D C3)
→ 27, rue Malar (7th)
Tel. 01 47 05 86 89
Closed Sun.
The photos hanging on the walls tell you that you have entered Basque country. Friendly service with an eclectic clientele. The south-west French cuisine includes: magret of duck, Spanish omelette, and Basque gâteau. Daily specials 74–92F; à la carte 180F, set menu 99F.

Noura (D B2)
→ 21–27, ave. Marceau (16th) Tel. 01 47 23 02 20
Daily until midnight.
One of the best Lebanese restaurants in Paris. Plates of *meze* at 68F, *chawarma* chicken-tabouleh 84F and pastries 24F. Excellent wine list, all available by the glass.

Le Bistrot de Marius Rive Gauche (D D4)
→ 74, bd de la Tour-Maubourg (7th)
Tel. 01 47 53 80 86
Daily noon–2.30pm, 7–10.30pm.
This is one of the best fish restaurants in Paris: very fresh produce and simple, delicious dishes. Even better: it is open on Sun. Entrées 48F, main course up to 145F, desserts c.38F.

Tampopo (D A2)
→ 66, rue Lauriston (16th)
Tel. 01 47 27 74 52
Closed Sat lunch and Sun.
Nothing like the hectic Japanese restaurants on Rue Ste-Anne. Here you remove your shoes at the door and step into an atmosphere of zen calm and serenity; ancient traditions of Japanese cooking. Set menus 90F and 120F at lunchtime, 150F dinner.

La Fermette Marbeuf 1900 (D C2)
→ 5, rue Marbeuf (8th)
Tel. 01 53 23 08 00
Daily noon–3pm, 7pm–midnight.
Gilbert Isaac's excellent kitchen serves traditional cooking in a stunning Art-Nouveau décor. Pleasant terrace and a truly good wine list. Set menu 180F.

MUSÉE DE L'HOMME

TROCADÉRO

ARC DE TRIOMPHE

PONT DE-
BIR-HAKEIM

AVENUE DE-
AVENUE DE LA-
PARC DU CHAMP DE - MARS

RUE GÉNÉRAL-FERRIÉ

AV. GUSTAVE-FERRIÉ

RUE MARGUERITE

QUAI

Pl. du G
Goura

DE LA

AVE.

CHAMP-DE-MARS
[R.E.R.]

TOUR EIFFEL ★
CHAMP-DE-MARS

AVENUE DE MONTESSU

RUE DE L'UNIVERSIT

RUE DE MONTTESSU

BRANLY

AVENUE

PONT
D'IÉNA

AVENUE DES

Place de
Varsovie

TROCADÉRO

DE NEW YORK

SEINE

NATIONS-UNIES

MUSÉE ★
DE L'HOMME

RUE FRESNEL

PONT

PASSERELLE
DEBILLY

PALAIS DE
TOKYO MUSÉE
D'ART MODERNE

MUSÉE
DE LA MARINE

TROCADÉRO

Place du
Trocadéro-
et du-
11-Novembre

PRÉSIDENT-WILSON

AVENUE DU

Place d'Iéna

RUE DE LONGCHAMP

IÉNA

AV. PIERRE-1er DE-

PALAIS
GALLIERA
MUSÉE
GUIMET

AV. D'IÉNA

AV.

AVENUE MARCEAU

RUE GALILÉE

RUE DE CHAILLOT

RUE DE BASSANO

RUE DE

AME
CATH
IN F

SERB

XVIe

AV. KLÉBER

RUE
ST-DIDIER

RUE
LÉO-
DELIBES

RUE
LUBECK

RUE DE
BOISSIÈRE

BOISSIÈRE

Pl. des États-
Unis

RUE DE BELLOY

AVENUE KLÉBER

RUE LAURISTON

RUE COPERNIC

RUE
LA
PÉROUSE

RUE
PAUL-VALÉRY

AVENUE MARCEAU

RUE GIRAUDOUX

RUE DE PRESBOURG

AVENUE D'IÉNA

CENTRE DE
CONFÉRENCES
INTERNATIONALES

AVENUE VICTOR-HUGO

RUE LAURISTON

KLÉBER

ARC DE
TRIOMPHE

AVENUE FOCH

OFFICE
TOURISME
AIR
FRANCE

R. DE PRESBOURG

RUE VERNET

RUE GALILÉE

R. CHAT

GEO

A

B

MUSÉE DE LA MARINE

TOUR EIFFEL
CHAMP-DE-MARS

★ **Arc de Triomphe** (**D** B1)
→ *Pl. du Général-de-Gaulle
(8th) Tel. 01 55 37 73 77
Summer: daily 9.30am–11pm
Winter: daily 10am–10.30pm.*
This huge neoclassical arch dating from the Napoleonic era dominates the Champs-Élysées. Magnificent view from the top. Under the platform a museum traces the building's history.

★ **Trocadéro** (**D** A3)
On a hilltop overlooking the Seine the two wings of the impressive Palais de Chaillot encircle the Trocadéro's esplanade. All year round this is a favorite spot for roller-skaters; in summer, the ornamental lakes and fountains become improvized swimming pools.

★ **Musée de la Marine** (**D** A3)
→ *17, pl. du Trocadéro (16th) Tel. 01 53 65 69 69
Wed-Mon 10am–5.50pm.*
First begun in the Louvre in 1937, it moved to the Palais de Chaillot in 1997. This museum is famous for its fascinating collection of model boats tracing the history of seafaring and for its beautiful collection of technical pieces.

★ **Musée de l'Homme** (**D** A3)
→ *Palais de Chaillot 17, pl. du Trocadéro (16th) (**D** A3)*
*Tel. 01 44 05 72 72
Wed-Mon 9.45am–5.15pm.*
Prehistory, anthropology, biology and ethnology are the themes tackled by this museum (which is part of the Museum of Natural History). Weaponry, jewelry costumes and sculpture are exhibited by geographical location and theme.

★ **Tour Eiffel / Champ-de-Mars** (**D** B4)
→ *Champ-de-Mars (7th) Summer: daily 9am–midnight Winter: daily 9.30am–11pm.*
The symbol of Paris, it was erected in 1889 for the World Exhibition. The Eiffel Tower was, at that time, the tallest building in Paris.

Now, including the ante on the top, this gigantic steel structure stands 1,053 ft high. From the t floor observatory, you ca see for 40 miles across Paris on a clear day. But is from the base that you get a real sense of its magnitude. At the foot o the tower, the Champ- de Mars park, (designed in 1908), stretches all the to the l'École Militaire. From there you get a stunning view of the Eiff Tower and the Trocadéro

★ **Palais de Tokyo / Musée d'Art Moderne la Ville de Paris** (**D** B2
→ *11, ave. Président-Wils*

D

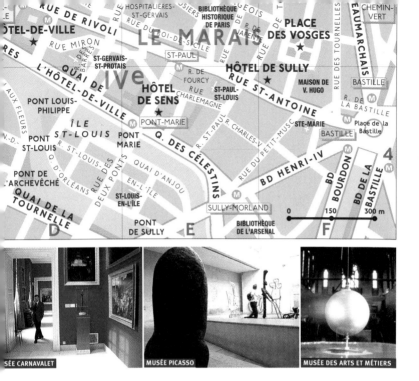

Map labels

RUE DE RIVOLI · HOSPITALIÈRES-ST-GERVAIS · RUE DU ROI-DE-SICILE · BIBLIOTHÈQUE HISTORIQUE DE PARIS · CHEMIN-VERT · PLACE DES VOSGES · BEAUMARCHAIS

ÔTEL-DE-VILLE · RUE MIRON · ST-GERVAIS-ST-PROTAIS · ST-PAUL · LE MARAIS · RUE DES FRANCS · RUE DE TURENNE · RUE DES TOURNELLES

QUAI DE L'HÔTEL-DE-VILLE · ST-PAUL · HÔTEL DE SENS · R. DE FOURCY · RUE CHARLEMAGNE · HÔTEL DE SULLY · RUE ST-ANTOINE · MAISON DE V. HUGO · BASTILLE

PONT LOUIS-PHILIPPE · ÎLE ST-LOUIS · PONT MARIE · ST-PAUL-ST-LOUIS · R. DE LA BASTILLE · Place de la Bastille · STE-MARIE · BASTILLE

PONT ST-LOUIS · Q. D'ORLÉANS · RUE DES DEUX PONTS · QUAI D'ANJOU · Q. DES CÉLESTINS · R. ST-PAUL · R. CHARLES-V · RUE DU PETIT-MUSC · BD HENRI-IV · BD BOURDON · BD DE LA BASTILLE

PONT DE L'ARCHEVÊCHÉ · QUAI DE LA TOURNELLE · ST-LOUIS-EN-L'ÎLE · PONT DE SULLY · SULLY-MORLAND · BIBLIOTHÈQUE DE L'ARSENAL

0 · 150 · 300 m

D · E · F · 4

SÉE CARNAVALET · **MUSÉE PICASSO** · **MUSÉE DES ARTS ET MÉTIERS**

Marais and was a ter of society life in the e of the dukes of Sully. e main courtyard, with Renaissance décor, the rden and the orangery all still intact. Today it he home of the Caisse ionale des Monuments toriques (state-funded ce which protects the tural heritage).

Place des Vosges E3)

ck façades, high French oles, arcaded galleries... sumptuous former ce Royale has retained the splendor of the days Henry IV's reign. At n° 6, tor Hugo's house has been turned into a little museum.

★ Hôtel de Soubise (C E3)
→ 60, rue des Francs-Bourgeois (3ʳᵈ)
Tel. 01 40 27 62 18
Mon, Wed-Fri 10am-5.45pm (from 1.45pm at weekends).
Built by Boffand in 1735, this is a Parisian *rocaille*-style masterpiece. The outside of the building, with its austere air, is in stark contrast to the extravant interior decor with its white and gold paneling and allegorical stucco *haut-reliefs* in the salon. The National Archives and the Museum of French History are now housed here.

★ Musée Carnavalet (C E3)
→ 23, rue de Sévigné (3ʳᵈ)
Tel. 01 44 59 58 58
Tue-Sun 10am-5.40pm.
Rich collection of art centered around Parisian history, archeology, architecture, society and culture.

★ Musée Picasso (C E3)
→ 5, rue de Thorigny (3ʳᵈ)
Tel. 01 42 71 25 21
Wed-Mon 9.30am-5.30pm (until 8pm Thu).
Superb Marais townhouse entirely dedicated to Picasso. It contains a chronological review of the work of the artist from 1894 to 1972. The scope of the works makes this the most important collection of Picasso's work in the world.

★ Musée des Arts et Métiers (C D1)
→ 60, rue Réaumur (3ʳᵈ)
Tel. 01 53 01 82 00
Tue-Sun 10am-6pm (until 9.30pm Thu).
Discover Pascal's calculating machine, Lavoisier's laboratory, Foucault's pendulum and 84,000 other objects and documents following the great technological inventions from the 16th century to the present day.

CHRISTIAN LACROIX CHANEL FAGUAIS

La Maison de l'Alsace (**D** C1)

➜ 39, ave. des Champs-Élysées (8th)
Tel. 01 53 93 97 00
Daily 24 hours.
This large brasserie on Champs-Élysées never closes and serves some of the best Alsatian food in Paris. Saeuerkraut, roasted suckling pig, incredibly fresh seafood platters. À la carte 250F.

TEAROOMS

Ladurée (**D** C1)

➜ 75, ave. des Champs-Élysées (8th)
Tel. 01 40 75 08 75
Daily 7.30am–1am.
Thirty flavors of macaroons including coffee, chocolate, vanilla, rose petal and Guérande caramel. All served against a backdrop of stucco, gilt and marble. Genteel service.
The other Ladurée is at 16, rue Royale (8th).
18F large macaron, 7.50F small.

CAFÉS, BARS, MUSIC VENUES

Café du Musée Rodin (**D** D4)

➜ 77, rue de Varenne (7th)
Tel. 01 45 50 42 34 Tue-

Sun 10am–6pm (4.30pm in winter).
Enjoy a pleasant drink or snack in the tranquil setting of the Rodin Museum statue garden. Entrance fee to the garden 5F.

Café Thoumieux (**D** C3)

➜ 4, rue de la Comète (7th) Tel. 01 45 51 50 40
Mon-Fri noon–2am; Sat 7pm–2am.
Red velvet décor enjoyed by a young sophisticated clientele. Excellent cocktails 50F, tapas 60F and a huge screen showing sports events.

Master's Bar (**D** C4)

➜ 64, ave. Bosquet (7th)
Tel. 01 45 51 08 99
Daily 5pm–2am.
Thierry Delamare's famous cocktails. Happy hour during the week from 5–7pm. Cocktails 48–58F.

Le Doobie's (**D** C2)

➜ 2, rue Robert-Estienne (8th) Tel. 01 53 76 10 76
Mon-Sat 6pm–2am; Sun noon–2am.
A favorite with the fashion set. Cozy and intimate. Cocktails 60F.

Au Dernier Métro (**D** A5)

➜ 70, bd de Grenelle (15th)
Tel. 01 45 75 01 23
Daily 6am–2am.
A bar in a colorful

quartier where you can choose between 10 different draught beers alongside friends and locals. Lively atmosphere, especially on soccer match nights! Excellent south-west French cuisine. Main course 58–90F.

Le Queen (**D** C1)

➜ 102, ave. des Champs-Élysées (8th)
Tel. 01 53 89 08 90
Daily midnight–dawn.
This major club is one of the best Parisian gay bars. Erotic dancing for men only on Thursday and Saturday.
Themed nights: 'Disco' (Mon), 'Private' (Tue), 'Secret' (Wed), 'French variety' (Thu), 'House' (Fri-Sat) and '1980-90s' (Sun).

Théâtre des Champs-Élysées (**D** C2)

➜ 15, ave. Montaigne (8th)
Tel. 01 49 52 50 50
Mon-Sat. Closed July–Aug.
Opera, lyric opera, chamber music (on Sundays the Orchestre National de France) and contemporary dance under the direction of Dominique Meyer. Tickets 40–450F.
The theater's rooftop restaurant, Maison Blanche '15 Montaigne' offers gastronomic food

and a breathtaking view of Paris.

SHOPPING

La Maison du Chocolat (**D** C1)

➜ 56, rue Pierre-Charron (8th) Tel. 01 47 23 38 25
Mon-Sat 10am–7.30pm.
Chocolate in all possible forms: macaroons, chocolate bars, candies, drinks, pastries ... Heaven on earth for chocoholics.

Faguais (**D** C2)

➜ 30, rue de La Trémoille (8th) Tel. 01 47 20 80 91
Mon-Sat 9.30am–7pm.
Traditional-style grocery store. More than 2,000 kinds of produce made by traditional methods: Montélimar nougat, Agen prunes, Calissons d'Aix (almond paste sweets), teas, preserves and 50 rare coffee blends.

Virgin Mega store (**D** C1)

➜ 52, ave. des Champs-Élysées (8th)
Tel. 49 53 50 00
Mon-Sat 10am–midnight, Sun and public holidays noon–midnight.
In a lovely 1930s building: books, music, videos and on the top floor the Virgin Café, where you can grab a bite to eat or just stop for a drink. Daily specials 50–60F, à la carte 150F.

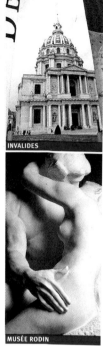

INVALIDES

MUSÉE RODIN

...th) Tel. 01 40 51 38 38
...e-Sun 10am–5.30pm.
...ened in 1961 inside
... Palais de Tokyo, the
...useum of Modern Art of
... City of Paris contains a
...perb collection of works
... Matisse, Dufy, Braque,
...d Picasso. Each year it
... a huge exhibition
...sed around a particular
...ist or theme.

Palais de la
couverte (D D2)
...Ave. Franklin-Roosevelt
...) Tel. 01 56 43 20 21
...-Sat 9.30am–5.30pm;
... 10am–6.30pm.
...vely approach to
...rning about science via
...ious interactive exhibits.

★ **Petit Palais** (D D2)
→ 1, ave. Winston-Churchill
(8th) Tel. 01 42 65 12 73
Tue-Sun 10am–5.40pm.
Home to Paris' Beaux-Arts
Museum (closed until
2002) and a site for large
temporary exhibitions.

★ **Grand Palais** (D D2)
→ Ave. Winston-Churchill
(8th) Tel. 01 44 13 17 17
Wed 10am–10pm;
Thu-Mon 10am–8pm.
The Grand Palais, partially
closed for building work,
houses large temporary art
exhibitions.

★ **Invalides/Musée**
de l'Armée (D D4)
→ Esplanade des Invalides
(5th) Tel. 01 44 42 37 67

Daily 10am–6pm (5pm in
winter).
The golden dome can be
seen for miles. Built for
Louis XIV in 1671-6, the
building served as a
hospital for the wounded
king's soldiers. Today the
Invalides contains the
Musée de l'Ordre de la
Libération, the church of
Saint-Louis and the tomb
of Napoleon I. A large part
of the war museum's
collection consists of
weaponry and items from
the collection of Napoleon
III.

★ **Musée Rodin** (D D4)
→ 77, rue de Varenne (7th)
Tel. 01 44 18 61 10

Tue-Sun 9.30am–4.45pm
(3.45pm in winter).
One of the most appealing
museums in Paris, this was
once Rodin's home and
workshop. It was converted
into a museum two years
after his death. Around
500 sculptures and 8000
photographs and drawings
by the artist are exhibited
here by rotation. Some of
Rodin's most important
works, including Le
Penseur (The Thinker), La
Porte de l'enfer (The Gates
of Hell) and Les Bourgeois
de Calais (The Burghers of
Calais) are on display in the
garden, under the shade of
the lime trees.

ÉGLISE SAINT-PIERRE

PLACE DU TERTRE

★ **Cimetière de Montmartre** (**E** A3)
→ *20, ave. Rachel (18th)*
Tel. 01 43 87 64 24
Daily 9am–5.45pm
The undulating countryside, the 100-year-old trees and the beautiful statues are all reminiscent of the Père-Lachaise cemetery. In this romantic setting lie the remains of, among others, Berlioz, Offenbach, Zola Fragonard, Vigny, Sacha Guitry, A. Dumas, Nijinsky and François Truffaut. Thirteen years after her death, flowers and poems are still left every day on the tomb of the singer Dalida who lived nearby.

★ **Musée de Montmartre** (**E** C3)
→ *12, rue Cortot (18th)*
Tel. 01 46 06 61 11
Tue-Sun 11am–5.30pm.
A complete history of the quartier (cabarets, painters and singers) told via posters, paintings, music and photographs. Housed in a charming 17th-century house overlooking the vineyards.

★ **Sacré-Cœur** (**E** C3)
→ *35, rue du Chevalier-de-La-Barre (18th)*
Tel. 01 53 41 89 00
Daily 6am–11pm.
Symbol of la Butte and of a Paris now long gone, this church with its Romanesque-Byzantine silhouette is an integral part of the Montmartre landscape. It was declared a public utility by the Chamber of Deputies from 1875 to 1919. It offers the best views of Paris (from the steps and from the dome itself).

★ **Église Saint-Pierre-de-Montmartre** (**E** C3)
→ *2, rue du Mont-Cenis (18th) Tel. 01 46 06 57 63*
Mon-Sat 8.30am–7.30pm (6.30pm Sun).
One of the oldest churches in Paris, hidden behind an 18th-century façade. This is all that now remains of the Abbaye aux Dames (1147), erected on what are presumed to be the rema of an ancient Gallo-Roma temple; the four marble columns in the choir probably date from this time. Beneath the choir and the transept lies the tombstone of its founder Queen Adélaïde.

★ **Place du Tertre** (**E** C
Street artists specializin in portraits or caricature a mass of easels, flocks tourists … this former square of the old village has become a Montmar cliché. But in the early morning when the squa is at its quietest, it is ve pleasant to have coffee

E

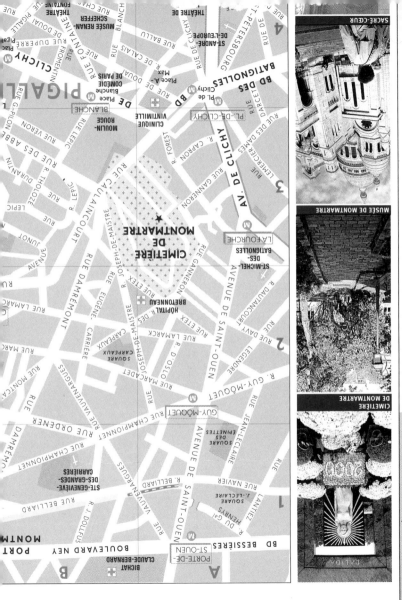

SACRÉ-CŒUR

MUSÉE DE MONTMARTRE

CIMETIÈRE DE MONTMARTRE

The Sacré-Cœur, perched at the top of La Butte, attracts tourists from all over the world. The artists, cabarets and balls of the Belle Époque may be long gone but the old charm of Montmartre lives on in the steep streets, stairways and pretty, ivy-covered houses. As evening falls the concert halls on the boulevards fill up and the sex scene in Pigalle begins to come to life. Two minutes away the Nouvelle Athène entices visitors with the romantic charm of its quiet little streets and Directoire-style architecture – an oasis in the midst of the bustle of the big boulevards.

BOUILLON CHARTIER

L'ÉTÉ EN PENTE DOUCE

RESTAURANTS

Le Zouave Gobichon (**E** B3)
→ 8, rue Durantin (18ᵗʰ)
Tel. 01 46 06 25 75
Closed Sun lunch and Mon.
Small, cozy dining room serving good quality, varied French cuisine. Zouave often invites local artists to exhibit their works here. Vegetarian special 69F.

L'Été en Pente Douce (**E** B2)
→ 23, rue Muller (18ᵗʰ)
Tel. 01 42 64 02 67. Daily.
Restaurant and tearoom with a large terrace. Salads 48–56F, traditional dishes 72–95F. Seasonal and vegetarian menus.

Bouillon Chartier (**E** C6)
→ 7, rue du Faubourg-Montmartre (9ᵗʰ)
Tel. 01 47 70 86 29. Daily 11.30am–3pm, 6–10pm.
Superb Belle Époque canteen serving cheap, straightforward cooking in the midst of a pleasant hubbub. Set menu 78F.

Le Mono (**E** B3)
→ 40, rue Véron (18ᵗʰ)
Tel. 01 46 06 99 20
Mon-Tue and
Thu-Sun 7–11.30pm
(lunch by reservation).
Typical décor, music and food from Togo. Specialties include:

gbekui (smoked fish in spinach sauce), chicken djenkoumé (half wheat, half corn-meal pastry) and braised fish in moyo (mild spices). À la carte 100F.

Per Bacco (**E** D3)
→ 10, rue Lambert (18ᵗʰ)
Tel. 01 42 52 22 40
Mon-Fri noon–2.30pm,
8–10.30pm; Sat 8–10.30pm.
The Naples-born chef of this restaurant has his produce sent direct from Italy. Authentic cuisine in an unpretentious setting. Attentive service.
À la carte 200F.

Beauvilliers (**E** C2)
→ 52, rue Lamarck (18ᵗʰ)
Tel. 01 42 54 54 42.
Closed Sun and Mon lunch.
The most prestigious restaurant on la Butte, run by maître d' Édouard Carlier. Elegantly imaginative gastronomy: grilled red mullet in fine escabèche (marinaded and served cold), artichoke hearts stuffed with crab. Set menu 185F lunch, 400F dinner (including wine).

BARS, CLUBS, CABARET

Le Sancerre (**E** B3)
→ 35, rue des Abbesses (18ᵗʰ) Tel. 01 42 58 08 20
This trendy café-bar is

JLIN-ROUGE   PRINTEMPS   ART'S FACTORY

located in the heart of the Abbesses district. At its best in the late afternoon and evening when the terrace is inundated with locals.

La Fourmi (**E** C5)
→ 74, rue des Martyrs (18th) Tel. 01 42 64 70 35
Daily 8am–2am.
Café situated at the crossroads of the trendy section of Pigalle, and near La Cigale, the famous concert hall (*La cigale et la fourmi* is one of La Fontaine's *Fables*). Good crowd and a fashionable place to be seen. Ideal for breakfast or a snack (salads, sandwiches and daily specials).

Élysée-Montmartre (**E** C4)
→ 72, bd Rochechouart (18th) Tel. 01 55 07 06 00
Originally a ballroom (1807) this has become a leading light on the Paris dance scene. Fans of alternative rock or world music sway under the 1900s molding. Live band and DJ every other Sat.

Divan du Monde (**E** C5)
→ 75, rue des Martyrs (18th) Tel. 01 44 92 77 66
World music (African, Brazilian, Caribbean, Oriental) and also themed evenings, films

and dance in this former Belle Époque cabaret venue.

Rex Club (**E** D6)
→ 5, bd Poissonnière (2nd) Tel. 01 42 36 10 96
Wed-Sat 11am–dawn.
Parisian home of electronic music presided over by the best DJs of the moment.

Moulin-Rouge (**E** B4)
→ 82, bd de Clichy (18th) Tel. 01 53 09 82 82
Daily 7pm (dinner); 9pm, 10pm, (shows).
A Paris institution! Reservation essential.

Max Linder (**E** C6)
→ 24, bd Poissonnière (9th) Tel. 01 48 24 00 47
1930s Art-Deco cinema. Large screen, state-of-the-art sound system and a bar on the ground floor.

SHOPPING

Art's Factory (**E** C4)
→ 48, rue d'Orsel (18th) Tel. 01 53 28 13 50
Tue-Sat 11am–7.30pm; Sun 2–7pm.
Dynamic art gallery exhibiting – and selling – contemporary works (paintings, sculpture, photos, objects etc.). Their mission is to promote 'Cheap Art', art which is within everyone's price range.

Patricia Louisor (**E** C4)
→ 16, rue Houdon (18th) Tel. 01 42 62 10 42
Daily noon–8pm.
Young stylist in the heart of the fashionable square delineated by Pigalle-Abbesses-Anvers. Fashion that is imaginative, original and also affordable.

Pain d'Épice (**E** C6)
→ 29 passage Jouffroy (2nd) Tel. 01 47 70 08 68
Mon 12.30–7pm; Tue-Sun 10am–7pm.
A most amazing toy store. Ancient dolls, accessories for children's parties, wooden mobiles, cots, trains, miniature soldiers and collectors' items.

Department stores (**E** A6)

Le Printemps
→ 64, bd Haussmann (9th) Mon-Sat 9.35am–7pm (until 10pm Thu).

Les Galeries Lafayette
→ 40, bd Haussmann (9th) Mon-Sat 9.30am–6.45pm (until 9pm Thu).
The two best department stores on the Boulevard. Printemps boasts stucco, Belle Époque, Art Deco, and listed 19th-century glass. Top brand names, accessories and an astonishing range of services. Lafayette Gourmet, next door,

is a favorite with foodies and wine lovers. Grab a bite there (tastings every lunchtime) or take out.

Tati (**E** D4)
→ 4, bd Rochechouart (18th) Tel. 01 55 29 50 00
Mon–Sat 10am–7pm.
www.tati.fr
Open in 1948, this is the first of the Tati stores. 'The lowest prices' in town and guaranteed entertainment!

Marché St-Pierre (**E** C3)
→ 2, rue Charles-Nodier (18th) Tel. 01 46 06 92 25
Mon 1.30–6.30pm; Wed-Sat 10am-6.30pm.
Truly the best place to buy fabric, attracting sewing enthusiasts, designers and interior decorators. Over a 2,400-sq-yds area flannel, tweed, silk, linen, cotton, ticking, sequined and floral fabrics sold by the meter.

Puces de Saint-Ouen et Clignancourt (**E** C1)
→ Porte de Clignancourt (18th) Sat-Mon 9.30am–7pm
The oldest and largest of Parisian flea markets: 2,000 outlets, 9 miles to walk and 150,000 visitors each week! Bric-à-brac and specialist markets: Biron (antiques), Malik (fashion), Malassis (art), Serpette (second-hand goods) ...

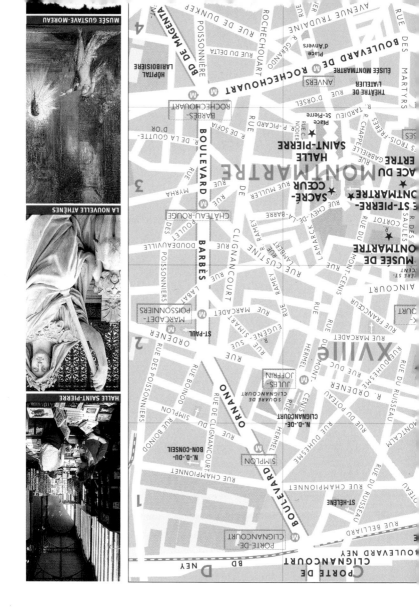

MUSÉE GUSTAVE-MOREAU

LA NOUVELLE ATHÈNES

HALLE SAINT-PIERRE

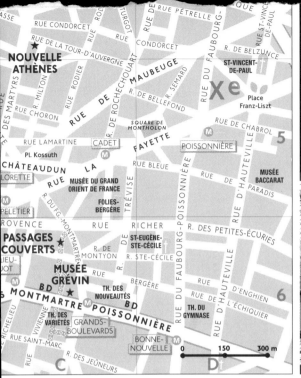

MUSÉE GRÉVIN

PASSAGE JOUFFROY

e terrace of La Mère
therine, a bistro which
as already popular during
e time of the French
volution.

La Nouvelle Athènes
C4)
e triangle formed by
ace Pigalle/Notre-Dame-
-Lorette/Sainte-Trinité
s built in the 18th
ntury and is full of
mantic splendor:
glish gardens, court-
rds, vaulted passage-
ays, and neoclassical
ildings where a presti-
us community of artists
ce lived and worked
erlioz, Sand, Degas,
opin, Dumas...).

★ **Halle Saint-Pierre**
(**E** C3)
→ 2, rue Ronsard (18th)
Tel. 01 42 58 72 89
Daily 10am–6pm.
Small glass and iron-
covered marketplace dating
from 1868. Since 1986 it
has housed the Musée
d'Art Naïf Max-Fourny
which exhibits primitive art
by artists from all over the
world. Pleasant tearoom on
the ground floor.
★ **Musée Gustave-
Moreau** (**E** B5)
→ 14, rue de La
Rochefoucauld (9th)
Tel. 01 48 74 38 50
Mon & Wed 11am–5.15pm;
Thu–Sun 10am–12.45pm,

2–5.15pm.
Around 5,000 drawings
and 1,200 paintings by the
Symbolist painter Gustave
Moreau (including Jupiter
et Sémélé) on show in his
former mansion-studio,
which was turned into a
museum in 1902.
★ **Musée Grévin** (**E** C6)
→ 10, bd Montmartre (9th)
Tel. 01 47 70 85 05
Daily 1–6.30pm (from 10am
during school holidays).
Several hundred celebrities,
influential and historical
figures immortalized as
waxworks. This museum,
was opened in 1882 by
journalist Arthur Meyer and
caricaturist Alfred Grévin.

★ **Covered Walkways**
(**E** C6)
→ Jouffroy, Verdeau and the
Panoramas passageways
10–11, bd Montmartre (2nd)
It took architectural sleight
of hand to build this superb
series of glass-covered
passageways and conceal
the irregularities of the site.
Panoramas opened in 1799,
followed by Jouffroy and
Verdeau in 1846 and 1847.
The various stores have
changed very little. Some
of the shop windows are
almost miniature museums
in their own right filled with
books, comics, toys, old
cameras ... plus tearooms
and restaurants. A gem.

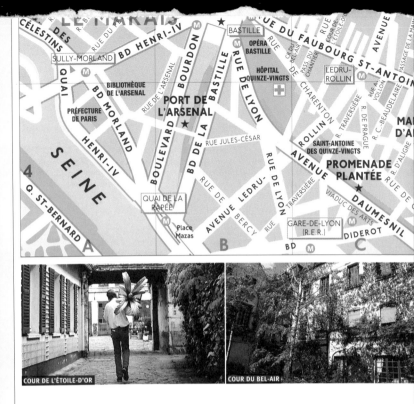

COUR DE L'ÉTOILE-D'OR

COUR DU BEL-AIR

★ Cimetière du Père-Lachaise (F F2)
→ 16, rue du Repos (19th)
Tel. 01 55 25 82 10 Daily
8am–6pm (5.30pm in winter)
Shaded avenues, under-growth, winding paths, esplanades... this cemetery (1804) is like a miniature world. At bends in the path stand the most extravagant of tombs. Pyramids and Greek temples stand alongside more modest burial sites. Edith Piaf, Paul Eluard, Frédéric Chopin, Honoré de Balzac, Molière and Jim Morrison among others, rest in this fascinating garden of the dead.

★ Cirque d'Hiver (F B1)
→ 110, rue Amelot (11th)
Tel. 01 47 00 28 81
This extremely beautiful and colorful circus, built by Hittorff and opened by Napoleon III in 1852, has had an eventful past. Concerts, equestrian acts and even olympic shows have taken place here. Acquired by the Bouglione brothers in 1934, it has since been partially returned to its original purpose.

★ Boulevard Richard-Lenoir (F B2)
At the port of Arsenal, the canal enters into a long tunnel, surfacing a mile further, level with Rue du Faubourg-du-Temple. In 1859 Haussmann decided to build a platform over the canal and 15 little squares. Renovation work between 1993 and 1996 gave birth to a succession of gardens, fountains and contemporary-style playgrounds. On Thursdays and Sundays a wonderful food market is held between Place de la Bastille and Bréguet-Sabin métro.

★ Place de la Bastille (F B3)
The storming of this 14th-century fortress caused this square, in the course of the 19th century, to become the symbol of the French Revolution. At its center, the July column stands in homage to the victims of the *Trois Glorieuses* (the three-day Revolution of July 1830). The walkways of the Opéra district and the numerous terraced bars all around the square are always bustling.

★ Port de l'Arsenal (F B
Since 1983, the Bassin ha housed an attractive port which each year sees 1,300 vessels pass through. On the east ban a terraced garden stretche from the Bastille to the

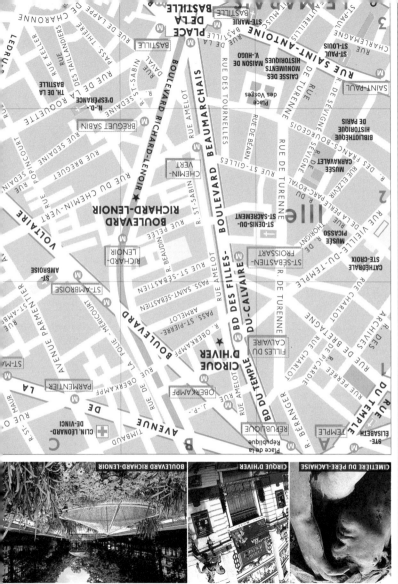

Place de la Bastille is where the capital's dedicated nightlife begins. Cafés, bars and restaurants line the surrounding streets: Rue du Faubourg-St-Antoine, Rue de la Roquette, Rue de Lappe and Rue de Charonne. But carry on further west along the Rue du Faubourg-St-Antoine and take a peek at the maze of courtyards and passageways. Cabinet-makers, for whom this area is renowned, now live alongside designers, architects, graphic designers and stylists. The Oberkampf area, north of Bastille, has now become the hippest, trendiest place to hang out in Paris, attracting nightowls on the prowl for new haunts.

LES AMOGNES   JACQUES MÉLAC

RESTAURANTS

Paris Main d'Or (F C3)
→ 133, rue du Faubourg-Saint-Antoine (11th)
Tel. 01 44 68 04 68
Mon-Sat noon–3pm, 8–11pm.
Tasty rustic cooking from Corsica: vegetables stuffed with *broccio* cheese, roast goat with potatoes. Set lunch menu 69F, Corsican specialties à la carte.

L'Ébauchoir (F D4)
→ 45, rue de Cîteaux (12th)
Tel. 01 43 42 49 31
Mon-Sat noon–2.30pm, 8–11pm.
A restaurant reflecting the local craft industry. Simple but good fare: lentil salad, beef *bourguignon*, crème caramel. 3-course lunch menu (incl. wine) 70F.

La Mère Lachaise (F E1)
→ 78, bd de Ménilmontant (20th) Tel. 01 47 97 61 60
Daily 8am–midnight.
Subdued décor extending onto the large terrace. On the menu, mixed salads, pies and daily specials.
À la carte 90F.

**Le Square Trousseau
(F** C4)
→ 1, rue Antoine-Vollon (11th) Tel. 01 43 43 06 00
Daily noon–2.30pm, 8–11.30pm.

This attractive bistro offers straightforward cooking, using the best market produce; it caters to a trendy, chic, local clientele. Excellent wine list. À la carte 200F.

Chez Paul (F C3)
→ 13, rue de Charonne (11th) Tel. 01 47 00 34 57
Daily noon–2.30pm, 7pm–midnight.
An institution in the quartier, nestled behind the crumbling exterior of an old house in the Rue de Charonne. Seafood salad with *foie gras*, grilled peppered steak.
À la carte 160F.

Les Amognes (F E4)
→ 243, rue du Faubourg-Saint-Antoine (11th)
Tel. 01 43 72 73 05
Mon 7.30–10.30pm;
Tue-Sat noon–2pm, 7.30–10.30pm (until 11pm Sat)
Fresh marinated sardine tart, sautéed squid with garlic and vegetables, crêpe stuffed with eggplant and cardamon. Thierry Coué's kitchen presents seasonal cooking which is both affordable and of good quality. Set menu 180F.

Chardenoux (F D3)
→ 1, rue Jules Vallès (11th)
Mon-Fri noon–2pm, 8–10pm; Sat 8–10.30pm.
Shiny moldings and a

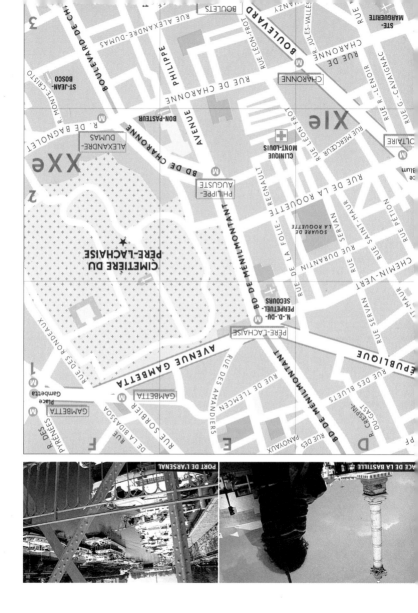

Map labels

3

RUE ALEXANDRE-DUMAS
BOULETS
RUE
STE-
MARGUERITE

BOULEVARD DE CH

BOULEVARD DE CHARONNE

RUE DE CHARONNE

RUE LÉON-FROT

RUE JULES-VALLÈS

LANZY

CHARONNE Ⓜ

RUE R.-LENOIR
RUE G.-CAVAIGNAC

ST-JEAN-
BOSCO

R. MONTAGEON

R. DE BAGNOLET

PHILIPPE

AVENUE PHILIPPE

RUE DE CHARONNE

BON-PASTEUR

RUE MERCŒUR

RUE LÉON-FROT

XIe

OLTAIRE

XXe

ALEXANDRE-
DUMAS

BD DE CHARONNE

PHILIPPE-
AUGUSTE Ⓜ

CLINIQUE
MONT-LOUIS ✚

RUE DE LA ROQUETTE

RUE REGNAULT

SQUARE DE
LA ROQUETTE

RUE DURANTIN

RUE SERVAN

RUE SAINT-MAUR

RUE PÉTION

CHEMIN-VERT

3lum
ce

2

★ CIMETIÈRE DU
PÈRE-LACHAISE

BD DE MÉNILMONTANT

RUE DE LA FOLIE-

T-MAUR

RUE DES RONDEAUX

N.-D.-DU-
PERPÉTUEL-
SECOURS ✚

PÈRE-LACHAISE Ⓜ

RUE SERVAN

RUE DES BLUETS

R. DUGAST

R. CRESPIN-

PF

1

Ⓜ GAMBETTA
Place
Gambetta

AVENUE GAMBETTA

RUE DE LA BIDASSOA

RUE SORBIER

RUE DES AMANDIERS

GAMBETTA Ⓜ

RUE DE TLEMCEN

AVENUE DE MÉNILMONTANT

BD DE MÉNILMONTANT

ÉPUBLIQUE

R. DES
PYRÉNÉES

RUE DES
PANOYAUX

D

F

E

D

Photo captions

PORT DE L'ARSENAL

ACE DE LA BASTILLE

LA BAGUE DE KENZA | VIADUC DES ARTS | BO PLASTIC

long counter... an old bistro that will take you back in time. Classic cuisine, complimented by inventive specialties (sweet and sour tarts with spiced *confit* of lamb). À la carte 250F.

Blue Elephant (**F** C3)
→ *43, rue de la Roquette (11th) Tel. 01 47 00 42 00 Closed Sat lunch.*
A tropical paradise: teak wood paneling, luxuriant greenery, Thaï orchids, a fountain splashing gently in the background. Excellent Thai cuisine. À la carte 250F.

CAFÉS, BARS, OPERA

Jacques Mélac (**F** E3)
→ *42, rue Léon-Frot (11th) Tel. 01 43 70 59 27 Mon 9am–5pm; Tue-Sat 9am–midnight.*
Vines trail over the front of Chez Mélac. Drinking water here is strongly discouraged! Wine, 20-25F a glass, is accompanied by plates of *charcuterie* from the Aveyron region (55F), cheese from Cantal or a hot dish.

Le Café du Passage (**F** C3)
→ *12, rue de Charonne (11th) Tel. 01 49 29 97 64 Daily noon–2am.*

English décor. Snacks and excellent wines, whiskies and champagne.

L'Entrepôt (**F** C3)
→ *14, rue de Charonne (11th) Tel. 01 48 06 57 04 Daily until 2am.*
Iron staircase, sofas, old photographs hanging on the walls and atmospheric music playing in the background. Cocktails: Happy Hour from 5 till 8.30pm.

Le Lèche-Vin (**F** B3)
→ *13, rue Daval (11th) Tel. 01 43 55 98 91 Tue-Thu 6pm–1am (until 2am Fri-Sat).*
Religious souvenirs of all sorts – icons of the Virgin Mary, Christ and the saints – along with draught beer, loud music and a young clientele ... The décor even extends to the W.Cs!

Le Café Charbon (**F** C1)
→ *109, rue Oberkampf (11e) Tel. 01 43 57 55 13 Daily until 2am.*
Industrial-style décor (gas lamps, zinc bar) and a very trendy clientele. À la carte 130F.

Les Couleurs (**F** C1)
→ *117, rue Saint-Maur (11th) Tel. 01 43 57 95 61 Daily until 2am.*
The look here is resolutely grunge, with non-matching formica

tables and old nicotine-stained walls. Lemon punch all day.

Le Balajo (**F** C3)
→ *9, rue de Lappe (11th) Tel. 01 47 00 07 87 Wed-Sun.*
Opened in 1936, the 'Bal à Jo' revives the tradition of the tea dance, with live accordion music every Thursday and Sunday. There are classes in Argentinian tango during the week as well as rock 'n' roll or salsa classes in the evening. Kitsch 1930s setting.

Opéra Bastille (**F** B3)
→ *pl. de la Bastille (11th) Tel. 08 36 69 78 68 for information / reservations*
Opera, lyric opera, classical ballet. Reserve several weeks in advance.

SHOPPING

La Bague de Kenza (**F** C1)
→ *106, rue Saint-Maur (11th) Tel. 01 43 14 93 15 Daily 9.30am–9pm.*
The best Algerian pastries in Paris. Wide choice of breads and savory specialties.

Cooperativa Cisternino (**F** C1)
→ *108, rue Saint-Maur (11th) Tel. 01 48 01 05 02 Mon-Sat 10am–1.30pm, 4–8pm; Sun 10am–1.30pm.*
Reasonably priced

cheeses *(mozzarella pecorino, parmesan)* and quality *charcuterie* from the Iberian Peninsula.

Viaduc des Arts (**F** C4)
→ *ave. Daumesnil (12th)*
Ceramics, tapestry, sculpture, cabinetmaking, painting and much more: over 45 designers and highly skilled craft-workers occupy the vaults of this viaduct, renovated in 1990.

Galerie Gaultier (**F** C3)
→ *30, rue du Faubourg-Saint-Antoine (11th) Tel. 01 44 68 84 84 Mon-Sat 11am–7.30pm.*
Clothes and accessories by Jean-Paul, the *enfant terrible* of the French fashion world.

Bo Plastic (**F** C3)
→ *31, rue de Charonne (11th) Tel. 01 53 36 73 16 Mon-Sat 11am–8pm.*
Plastic creations, mostly from the 60s and 70s, for collectors or 60s design junkies. Exhibitions too.

FNAC Bastille (**F** B3)
→ *4, pl. de la Bastille (12th) Tel. 01 43 42 04 04 Mon-Sat 10am–8pm (until 10pm Wed and Fri).*
Unlike the other branches of FNAC, here music takes pride of place. Specialist service. Ticket booth for concerts.

MARCHÉ D'ALIGRE

PROMENADE PLANTÉE

rland bridge. The ginal Port de l'Arsenal, ned in 1806 between Seine and Canal St-rtin, allowed the nsportation of wood raftworkers in the bourg St-Antoine.

Faubourg int-Antoine (F D4)
rue du Faubourg-St-oine (11ᵗʰ/12ᵗʰ)
m 1471, this *faubourg* hered around the abbey rowing community of penters, joiners, gilders varnishers authorized vork freely, outside of constraints of any poration. An urban mmunity slowly grew up around the faubourg, where craftworkers remain. Several centuries of urbanization have shaped the lovely courtyard of l'Étoile-d'Or at n° 75 rue du Faubourg-St-Antoine. On the other side of the street, the Passage du Chantier reflects the continued craft-industry activity in the district. Next door, at n° 58, you can see the magnificent Bel-Air court-yard, now extremely over-grown, while at n° 74 there is the great courtyard of the Burgundians – its iron architecture influenced by the 19th-century industrial-ization of the area.

★ **Marché d'Aligre (F** C4)
→ *rue and place d'Aligre (12ᵗʰ) Tue–Sun 8am–1pm.*
From early morning the little Place d'Aligre is packed and you have to fight your way through the crowds to get to the fruit and vegetable stalls on Rue d'Aligre. On the square there are florists and stalls of bric-à-brac. In the Halle Beauvau, built in 1787, meat, dairy and *charcuterie* stallholders shout at the top of their voices touting for customers.
A delightful market, full of Mediterranean colors, and offering the lowest prices in the capital.

★ **Promenade Plantée or 'Coulée Verte' (F** C4)
→ *bd Diderot and ave. Daumesnil (12ᵗʰ)*
Laid out between 1988 and 1993, this walk stretches ¾ sq mile from the Bastille to the Bois de Vincennes. Passing over viaducts (including the Viaduct des Arts) and across foot-bridges, the pedestrian can see a succession of gardens, some elaborately planted, some left to grow wild. An astonishing walkway hangs suspended at window level. From the Jardin de Reuilly a cycle track takes you into the Bois de Vincennes.

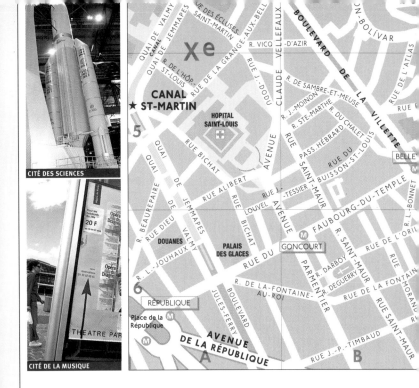

CITÉ DES SCIENCES

CITÉ DE LA MUSIQUE

Xe

QUAI DE VALMY
CANAL SAINT-MARTIN
QUAI DE JEMMAPES
RUE DE L'HÔP-
ST-LOUIS
RUE DE LA GRANGE-AUX-BELL
UE DES ÉCLUSES-
SAINT-MARTIN

R. VICQ
-D'AZIR
CLAUDE VELLEFAUX

BOULEVARD
ON-BOLIVAR

RUE DE L'ATLAS
-BOLIVAR

R. DE SAMBRE-ET-MEUSE
DE
LA VILLETTE
RUE F

**CANAL
★ ST-MARTIN**

R. J.-DODU
R. J.-MOINON
R. STE-MARTHE
PASS.-HÉBRARD
R. DU CHALET

RUE DU
BUISSON-ST-LOUIS

BELLE

**HÔPITAL
SAINT-LOUIS**

5

QUAI
DE
JEMMAPES

RUE BICHAT

RUE ALIBERT

AVENUE

RUE
SAINT-MAUR

RUE J.-
TESSIER-MAUR

FAUBOURG-DU-TEMPLE

R. L.-BONNET

BELLE

R. BEAUREPAIRE
R. L.-JOUHAUX
VALMY
RUE DIEU
DE
RUE J.-

DOUANES

BICHAT
LOUVEL
AVENUE

**PALAIS
DES GLACES**

RUE DU

GONCOURT Ⓜ

R. SAINT-MAUR
PARMENTIER
R. DARBOY
R. DEGUERRY

RUE DE L'ORI

RUE DE LA FONTAIN

MORAND

6

RÉPUBLIQUE

Place de la
République Ⓜ

R. DE LA-FONTAINE-
AU-ROI

BOULEVARD
JULES-FERRY

Ⓜ

AVENUE
DE LA RÉPUBLIQUE

RUE J.-P.-TIMBAUD

RUE SAINT-MAUR

THÉÂTRE PAR

A   B

★ Canal St-Martin (G A5)
Carved out between 1822
and 1825, at the request of
Napoleon I, to provide the
people of Paris with
drinking water, this canal
has become one of Paris'
most romantic spots. Its
planted banks and series
of locks, the metal foot
bridges and little gardens
that spread over 3 miles
are reminiscent of a Paris
that has now disappeared.
The legendary Hôtel du
Nord (immortalized in 1938
by Marcel Carné), was at
one time threatened with
destruction, but survived
and in 1996 was converted
into a restaurant.

**★ Parc de La Villette /
Canal de l'Ourcq (G** D1)
→ 221, ave. Jean-Jaurès (11th)
One of the most amazing
landscaped gardens in
Paris, completed in 1991,
on the site of the former
halles (covered market) of
La Villette. A decidedly
urban park, designed as a
'town garden' with main
thoroughfares, square,
walks and gardens. The
meadows of the Cercle
and the Triangle have a
total of 17 acres of grass.
The blue path of the
cinema promenade snakes
its way over nearly two
miles, crossing 10 themed
gardens. The park's lawns

come to life each summer
with concerts, displays and
a free open-air film festival
attracting huge audiences
from the city, longing to
be outdoors. A cycle track
offers a pleasant ride along
the Canal de l'Ourcq all the
way to Meaux, tens of
miles away.

**★ Cité des Sciences
et de l'Industrie (G** D1)
→ 30, ave. Corentin-Cariou
(19th) Tel. 01 40 05 80 00
Since 1986 this has
occupied the buildings of
the former slaughterhouses
and animal markets of La
Villette. The permanent
exhibition 'Explora'
consists of several displays

(space, the environment
the ocean, etc) organize
around one central area.
For children there are
participatory exhibits an
games, encouraging the
to literally come to grips
with scientific and techn
information, whilst 'Tech
Cité' focuses on the varic
different phases of an
industrial project. The
Géode building has an
hemispheric cinema scre
1,196 sq yards in size.

**★ Cité / Musée de
la Musique (G** D2)
→ Parc de la Villette
221, ave. Jean-Jaurès (19th
Tel. 01 44 84 45 45
This site is dedicated

G

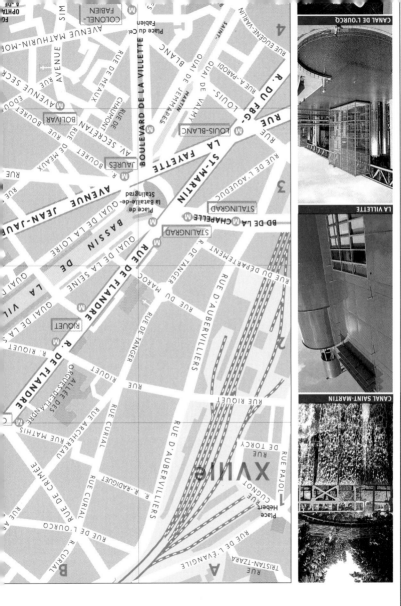

CANAL DE L'OURCQ

LA VILLETTE

CANAL SAINT-MARTIN

XVIIIe

Place Hébert

Place du Cel Fabien

Place de la Bataille-de-Stalingrad

BOULEVARD DE LA VILLETTE

AVENUE JEAN-JAURÈS

BD DE LA CHAPELLE

AVENUE MATHURIN-MOR

COLONEL-FABIEN

JAURÈS

STALINGRAD

LA FAYETTE

RUE DU FBG-ST-MARTIN

LOUIS-BLANC

RIQUET

RUE DE FLANDRE

R. DE FLANDRE

RUE EUGÈNE-VARLIN

QUAI DE JEMMAPES

QUAI DE VALMY

RUE A.-PARODI

RUE LOUIS-BLANC

RUE DE L'AQUEDUC

RUE DU DÉPARTEMENT

RUE DE TANGER

RUE DU MAROC

RUE DE TANGER

RUE D'AUBERVILLIERS

RUE RIQUET

RUE RIQUET

RUE CURIAL

RUE ARCHEREAU

RUE CURIAL

RUE CURIAL

R. DE CRIMÉE

RUE DE CRIMÉE

RUE MATHIS

ALLÉE DES ORGUES-DE-FLANDRE

RUE D'AUBERVILLIERS

RUE DE TORCY

RUE PAJOL

RUE DE L'ÉVANGILE

RUE TRISTAN-TZARA

RUE DE L'OURCO

R.-RADIGUET

CUGNOT

BASSIN DE LA VILLETTE

QUAI DE LA LOIRE

QUAI DE LA SEINE

QUAI DE LA S

RUE DE MEAUX

RUE DE CHAUMONT

AV. SECRÉTAN

RUE SECRÉTAN

AVENUE EDOU

RUE BOURET

RUE BOURET

AVENUE

RUE

OPHTA

FO

A DE

RUE DE MEAUX

Ménilmontant / Belleville / La Villette

Along the canals, Paris past and Paris present stand side by side. A walk along the banks of the Canal St-Martin is full of old-fashioned charm. The Canal de l'Ourq, by contrast, continues as far as La Villette, where a thoroughly 21st-century park suddenly appears out of nowhere. Further south the Park des Buttes-Chaumont, reformed in 1864 to rehabilitate the surrounding slum area, has given birth to a respectable residential district. Below it are the working-class villages of Belleville and Ménilmontant, rich with the influence of immigrants from Asia and the Orient.

LE BARATIN

RESTAURANTS

Benesti (**G** C6)
→ 108, bd de Belleville (20ᵗʰ) Tel. 01 44 55 44 55 Tue-Sun.
Wonderful Jewish Tunisian snacks: falafel sandwiches, *brik*, *choudchouka*, Tunisian salads, mint tea and pastries. A place where people eat lots and talk even more! An extra-ordinary taste of the Mediterranean.
Dinner 50–70F

Le Baratin (**G** C5)
→ 3, rue Jouye-Rouve (20ᵗʰ) Tel. 01 43 49 39 70 Tue-Sat noon–2.30pm, 8.30–11.30pm.
Impressive wine list compiled by patron Olivier Camus (there are 200 different wines on the menu). Excellent cuisine based around seasonal availability. Friendly atmosphere, unpretentious setting.
Lunch menu 73F.

La Boulangerie (**G** D6)
→ 15, rue des Panoyaux (20ᵗʰ) Tel. 01 43 58 45 45 Daily except Sat lunch.
This restaurant at the front of a traditional bakery, opened its doors in May 1999. The décor is as delicious as the cooking: *effilochade* of

dried duck with cardamom and creamed lentils, salt beef followed by Ménilmontant tart for dessert. Set menu, lunch 68F, dinner 98F.

L'Heure Bleue (**G** D4)
→ 57, rue Arthur Rozier (19ᵗʰ) Tel 01 42 39 18 07 Mon-Fri noon–2.30pm, 7–10.45pm;
Sat eve only 7–10.45pm
Good traditional cuisine with a south west touch (duck *confit*, foie gras) but also a wide range of very good vegetarian dishes (vegetable ravioli, savoury tarts). Set menu 65F (lunchtime only); à la carte 120-150F.

L'Atlantide (**G** C3)
→ 7, ave. Laumière (19ᵗʰ) Tel. 01 42 45 09 81 Tue-Sun 7.30pm–midnight.
Dine here and sample the best Berber specialties: couscous of fine semolina served with a choice of sauce or fresh steamed vegetables. The meat is succulent, particularly the *tajine* dishes (with dried fruits or vegetables). À la carte 150F.

La Cave Gourmande (**G** D4)
→ 10, rue du Gᵃˡ-Brunet (19ᵗʰ) Tel. 01 40 40 03 30 Mon-Fri noon–2pm, 7–10pm.
Restaurant, delicatessen

J PASCALOU   MARCHÉ DE BELLEVILLE   ÉPICERIE LE CAIRE

and wine merchant where fine food is always on offer. The choice is somewhat limited, but the menu changes daily. Set menu only, 170F.

Krung Thep (G C5)
→ *93, rue Julien-Lacroix (20th) Tel. 01 43 66 83 74 Daily 6pm–midnight.*
It's difficult to imagine that behind these smoked-glass windows lurks one of the the best Thai restaurants in Paris. Exotic setting, efficient service and, above all, delicious food with subtle and unusual combinations of flavors: sweet salad with banana flower, wrapped chicken, *pat thaï* (noodles sautéed with shrimp)... If the place is full, go straight to Lao Siam, *49, rue de Belleville,* instead.

CAFÉS, BARS, MUSIC VENUES

La Maroquinerie (G D6)
→ *23, rue Boyer (20th) Tel. 01 40 33 30 60 Closed Sun.*
This fashionable venue, with its ultra-modern décor used to be an old leather workshop, tucked away in a courtyard. Its concerts, exhibitions readings and debates

encourage meetings between local inhabitants and artists. Daily specials 50–60F.

Lou Pascalou (G D6)
→ *14, rue des Panoyaux (20th) Tel. 01 46 36 78 10 Daily 9am–2pm.*
Understated, but cozy, a limited number of tables and a terrace, obliging waiters... A popular, no-nonsense place, like its regulars. Rock or world music concerts and, occasionally, theater evenings.

Le Soleil (G C6)
→ *136, bd de Ménilmontant (20th). Tel. 01 46 36 47 44 Daily until 2am.*
Four rows of tables on the terrace spill out onto the sidewalk, tempting passersby. Sip a mint tea, a *pastis,* or a draught beer. Attracts a friendly, mixed crowd.

Aux Folies (G C5)
→ *8, rue de Belleville (19th) Tel. 01 46 36 65 98 Daily 6am–midnight.*
The neon sign conjures up the old Belleville. Here, in the 1930s, a café-theater drew the biggest names, from Édith Piaf to Yves Montand. Amar, who has now taken over the venue, has kept the original

décor. An unpretentious place where you can have a drink at the bar, or on the terrace, and sit watching the world go by.

Cité de la Musique (G D2)
→ *Parc de La Villette 221, ave. Jean-Jaurès (19th) Tel. 01 44 84 45 00 Concerts 90–200F. www.cite-musique.fr*
An oval-shaped auditorium seating 800-1,200. Weekend concerts tend to be organized around a particular theme. Jazz classical, contemporary and traditional music concerts. There is also a multi-media library and information center on music and dance (Tue-Sun until 6pm).

Le Trabendo (G D2)
→ *211, ave Jean-Jaurès (20th) Tel. 01 42 54 07 47 for program information.*
Formerly known as Hot Brass, this auditorium seats 700 and is filled with the graffiti art of Futura 2000. Modern venue for rock, world music and jazz concerts. Entrance 80–120F.

SHOPPING

Marché de Belleville (G B5-C6)

→ *M° Belleville and Ménilmontant*
Every Tuesday and Friday the central divider strip of the Boulevard de Belleville plays host to one of the largest markets in Paris. Hundreds of colorful stalls selling fruit, vegetables, spices ... the crowds are extraordinary.

Épicerie Le Caire (G C5)
→ *63, rue de Belleville (19th) Tel. 01 42 06 06 01 Tue–Sun 10am–10pm.*
Adel Moussa's grocery store resembles a *souk*: olives, spices, cheese, rice, semolina and Egyptian specialties (cardamom-flavored coffee, *mammoul* with dates, pistachio or walnuts *borek* with cheese or spinach ...).

Nani (G D5)
→ *104, rue de Belleville (20th) Tel. 01 47 97 38 05 Sun–Fri 8am–7.30pm.*
Since 1962 Nani has made the locals salivate. The store's narrow front hides a small, long pâtisserie. On the left are classics like lemon tarts, strawberry gâteaux, *millefeuille* pastries... on the right, a mountain of oriental pastries: *makroud, baklava, oreillettes* with honey...).

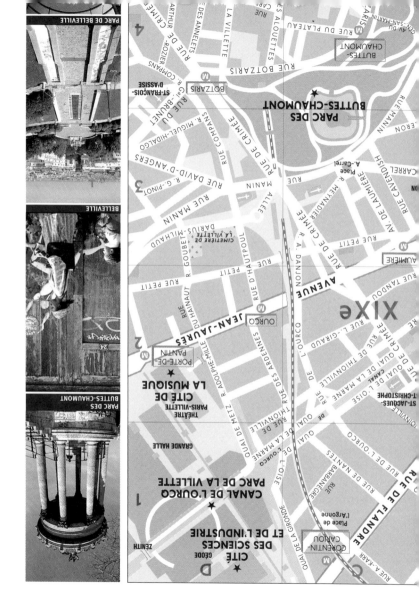

PARC DE BELLEVILLE

BELLEVILLE

PARC DES
BUTTES-CHAUMONT

PARC DES
BUTTES-CHAUMONT

PARC DE BELLEVILLE

★ St-François-
d'Assise

BUTTES-
CHAUMONT Ⓜ

RUE BOTZARIS

BOTZARIS Ⓜ

PARC DES
BUTTES-CHAUMONT ★

RUE DU PLATEAU

RUE ARTHUR-ROZIER

RUE DES ANNELETS

RUE DE CRIMÉE

RUE DE COMPANS

R. DU G⁺ BRUNET

R. MIGUEL-HIDALGO

RUE DE CRIMÉE

RUE COMPANS

RUE DAVID-D'ANGERS

R. G.-PINOT

3

RUE MANIN

RUE MANIN

RUE MANIN

ALLÉE

RUE MANIN

Place
A.-Carrel

R. MEYNADIER

AV. DE LAUMIÈRE

CARREL

RUE CAVENDISH

RUE PETIT

LAUMIÈRE Ⓜ

RUE PETIT

RUE D'HAUTPOUL

R. GOUBET

R. DARIUS-MILHAUD
CIMETIÈRE DE
LA VILLETTE

RUE PETIT

RUE DU HAINAUT

R. PETIT

RUE A. DANJON

AVENUE

JEAN-JAURÈS Ⓜ

2

★
CITÉ DE
LA MUSIQUE

THÉÂTRE
PARIS-VILLETTE

R. ADOLPHE-MILLE

RUE DES ARDENNES

PORTE-DE-
PANTIN Ⓜ

OURCQ Ⓜ

AVENUE

RUE DE L'OURCQ

RUE THIONVILLE

XIXᵉ

RUE L.-GIRAUD

RUE THIONVILLE

RUE DE CRIMÉE

RUE DE CRIMÉE

St-Jacques-
St-Christophe

RIONVILLE

QUAI DE L'OISE

RUE DE L'OURCQ

RUE DE NANTES

QUAI DE LA MARNE

QUAI DE L'OISE

GRANDE HALLE

★
CANAL DE L'OURCQ
PARC DE LA VILLETTE

QUAI DE METZ

RUE DE THIONVILLE

QUAI DE LA MARNE

RUE DE L'OURCQ

1

CITÉ
DES SCIENCES
ET DE L'INDUSTRIE
★
GÉODE

ZÉNITH

QUAI DE LA GIRONDE

Place de
l'Argonne

CORENTIN-
CARIOU Ⓜ

RUE
DE FLANDRE

RUE BARBANÈGRE

RUE A-KARR

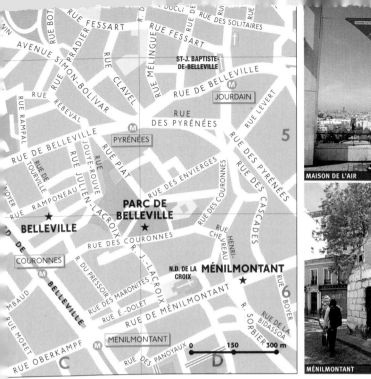

MAISON DE L'AIR

MÉNILMONTANT

Map labels:
- RUE BOT...
- RUE FESSART
- RUE PRADIER
- AVENUE SIMON-BOLIVAR
- RUE BOLIVAR
- RUE CLAVEL
- RUE MÉLINGUE
- RUE FESSART
- RUE DUCCI
- RUE DES SOLITAIRES
- ST-J. BAPTISTE-DE-BELLEVILLE
- RUE DE BELLEVILLE
- JOURDAIN
- RUE DES PYRÉNÉES
- RUE LEVERT
- 5
- RUE REBEVAL
- RUE RAMPAL
- RUE DE TOURVILLE
- RUE DE BELLEVILLE
- RUE JOUYE-ROUVE
- RUE PIAT
- RUE JULIEN-LACROIX
- PYRÉNÉES
- RUE DES ENVIERGES
- RUE DES COURONNES
- RUE DES PYRÉNÉES
- RUE DES CASCADES
- RUE RAMPONEAU
- ★ BELLEVILLE
- PARC DE BELLEVILLE ★
- RUE DES COURONNES
- RUE CHEVREAU
- RUE HENRI-
- COURONNES
- R. DU PRESSOIR
- BELLEVILLE
- R. J.-LACROIX
- N.D. DE LA CROIX
- MÉNILMONTANT ★
- MBAUD
- RUE MORET
- RUE DES MARONITES
- RUE É.-DOLET
- RUE DE MÉNILMONTANT
- RUE BOYER
- R. SORBIER
- RUE DE LA BIDASSOA
- 6
- MENILMONTANT
- RUE OBERKAMPF
- RUE DES PANOYAUX
- 0   150   300 m
- C
- D

music in all forms. ...ated to the south ...he Parc de La Villette, ...ouses the exclusive ...servatoire and ...oncert hall which stages ...certs throughout the ...r. The museum, opened ...997, acquires, restores ...l exhibits a collection ...what is now more than ...00 instruments dating ...n the Renaissance to ...present day.

**Parc des Buttes-
...aumont (G** C4)
→ *Rues Manin and Botzaris
...th) Daily 7.30am–11pm
...m in winter).*

...ginally part of Napoleon ...' desire to make Paris a

healthier place to live in, this park was renovated in 1864 taking over slum areas and giving the northeast of the capital its own large area of greenery. The architect Davioud transformed the former quarries, carving them into a lake and creating a series of waterfalls, streams, embankments and plantations. It is a stunning park where the paths plunge into the undergrowth, clamber up rocks and then, suddenly, open up onto higher land.

★ Belleville (G C6)
→ *Between rue and bd de
Belleville (19th / 20th)*

Even at dawn the Boulevard de Belleville is busy, with lively discussions and card games going on. The café-terraces are packed with people and from the surrounding stalls, the air is filled with the delicious smell of mint tea and the sound of oriental music. Rue de Belleville, which runs to the top of the hill, is a regular little Chinatown, while grocers, restaurants, cafés and bazaars run the length of the Rue des Pyrénées.

★ Parc de Belleville (G D6)
→ *Rue des Couronnes, rue
Piat and rue Jouye-Rouve (20th)*
Rue Piat, which in the 19th

century lead the way to two windmills, now emerges in a lovely park built on the buttresses of a former gypsum quarry. Spectacular views of the capital. Workshops and exhibitions at the Maison de l'Air (at the top of the park).

★ Ménilmontant (G D6)
→ *Rue de Ménilmontant (20th)*
These streets have not entirely lost their appeal: Rue des Cascades has charming houses and Rue de la Mare has a pretty track over the railway. Rue des Envierges takes you right back to the Parc de Belleville.

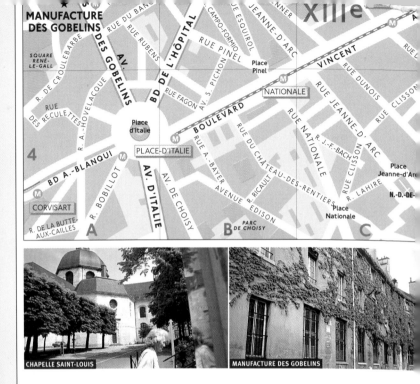

MANUFACTURE
DES GOBELINS

SQUARE
RENÉ-
LE-GALL

RUE DU BANQ
RUE RUBENS
RUE PINEL
CAMPO-FORMIO
JEANNE-D'ARC
RUE PINEL
Place
Pinel
RUE DE L'HÔPITAL
BD DE L'HÔPITAL
RUE FAGON
A. V. S. PICHON
RUE DES RÉCULETTES
R. A. HOVELACQUE
R. DE CROULEBARBE
AV. DES GOBELINS
RUE JEANNE-D'ARC
VINCENT
RUE DUNOIS
NATIONALE
BOULEVARD
Place
d'Italie
RUE NATIONALE
PLACE-D'ITALIE
RUE A. BAYER
RUE DU CHÂTEAU-DES-RENTIERS
R. J.-F.-BACH
RUE CLISSON
RUE CLISSON
R. LAHIRE
Place
Jeanne-d'Arc
BD A.-BLANQUI
R. BOBILLOT
AV. D'ITALIE
AV. DE CHOISY
AVENUE R. RICAULT-DES-RENTIERS
EDISON
N.-D.-DE-
CORVISART
R. DE LA BUTTE-
AUX-CAILLES
A
PARC
DE CHOISY
B
Place
Nationale
C

XIIIe

4

CHAPELLE SAINT-LOUIS

MANUFACTURE DES GOBELINS

★ Institut du Monde Arabe (H B1)
➜ 1, rue des Fossés-St-Bernard (5th)
Tel. 01 40 51 38 38
Daily 10am–6pm.
This amazing building designed by Jean Nouvel is an adaptation of an Arab-Hispanic architectural concept using contemporary materials. The museum is dedicated to the art and culture of Arab and Islamic civilizations, as is the library, specialist book-store and also the cinema, concerts, dance performances and temporary exhibitions.

★ Arènes de Lutèce (H A1)
➜ 49, rue Monge (5th) Daily.
Discovered in 1869 while clearing the Rue Monge, these remains of a Gallo-Roman amphitheater were later incorporated into a peaceful garden which has today become a sports field – a firm favorite with children and locals who like playing boules.

★ Muséum National d'Histoire Naturelle (H B2)
➜ 57, rue Cuvier (5th)
Tel. 01 40 79 30 00
Mon, Wed-Sun 10am–6pm (Thu until 10pm).
The Paleontology and Anatomy galleries of the Natural History Museum both resemble an 18th-century surgery, full of strange curiosities. They are also intact: waxed parquet floors, original windows and old, hand-written labels, providing fodder for a formidable tour of the human body and a fascinating journey through the world of fossils, dinosaur bones, giant birds and insects. In the Evolution gallery is a permanent exhibition on the evolution of life. The immense collection of stuffed animals on show in the nave is frighteningly lifelike and impressive in size.

★ Jardin des Plantes (H B2)
➜ Rue Cuvier, rue Buffon and place Valhubert (5th)
Tel. 01 40 79 30 00
Daily 10am–5pm.
Facing the Grande Galer the botanical garden and flower beds; on the right are two large glasshouse (Mexican and Tropical). large maze takes you pa rare species of plants, w the cries of various exoti animals can be heard fro the zoo. In 1635, the roy garden of medicinal plar became the first park in Paris to open its gates to

H

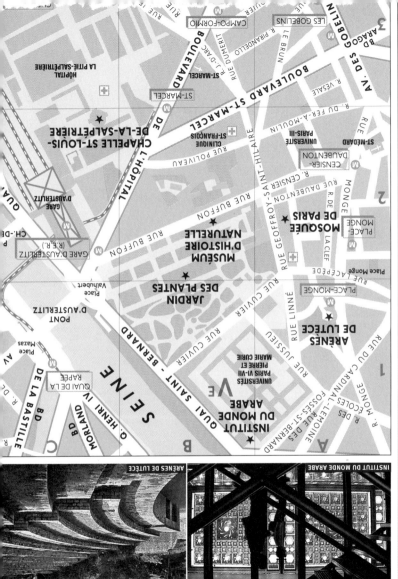

RUE ÉLIE

M CAMPO-FORMIO

LES GOBELINS M

BD ARAGO 3

BOULEVARD DE L'HÔPITAL

HÔPITAL
LA PITIÉ-SALPÉTRIÈRE

ST-MARCEL

ST-MARCEL M

R. DUMERIL

R. J. D'ARC

R. PIRANDELLO

LE BRUN

BOULEVARD ST-MARCEL

R. VESALE

AV. DES GOBELINS

CHAPELLE ST-LOUIS-
DE-LA-SALPÊTRIÈRE ★

RUE DE L'HÔPITAL

RUE POLIVEAU

CLINIQUE
ST-FRANÇOIS

UNIVERSITÉ
PARIS-III

R. DU FER-À-MOULIN

ST-MÉDARD

CENSIER-
DAUBENTON M

GARE
D'AUSTERLITZ

QUAI D'AUSTERLITZ

RUE BUFFON

RUE DAUBENTON

RUE CENSIER

RUE GEOFFROY-SAINT-HILAIRE

RUE DE MONGE

PLACE-
MONGE M

PLACE-MONGE

CH.-DE

GARE D'AUSTERLITZ
(R.E.R.) M

RUE BUFFON

MUSÉUM
D'HISTOIRE
NATURELLE ★

LA CLEF

MOSQUÉE
DE PARIS ★

RUE LACÉPÈDE

Place Monge

PONT
D'AUSTERLITZ

Place
Valhubert

JARDIN
DES PLANTES ★

RUE CUVIER

RUE LINNÉ

ARÈNES
DE LUTÈCE ★

M PLACE-MONGE

SEINE

QUAI SAINT - BERNARD

Place
Mazas

AV

DE LA RAPÉE

QUAI DE LA RAPÉE

R. DE

RUE CUVIER

UNIVERSITÉS
PARIS VI-VII
PIERRE ET
MARIE CURIE

RUE JUSSIEU

RUE DU CARDINAL-LEMOINE

INSTITUT
DU MONDE
ARABE ★

RUE DES FOSSÉS-ST-BERNARD

R. DES
ÉCOLES

R. MONGE

RUE DU CARDINAL-LEMOINE

O. HENRI IV

Q. MORLAND

BD
MORLAND

BD
DE LA BASTILLE

R. DE

ARÈNES DE LUTÈCE

INSTITUT DU MONDE ARABE

Place d'Italie / Bibliothèque Nationale / Bercy

The immense Bibliothèque Nationale (1997) is seen as a symbol for the east side of Paris, an area which has totally changed over the past two decades. The industrial wastelands of Bercy and Austerlitz have provided architects and town planners with invaluable experimental freedom, resulting in the Institut du Monde Arabe in 1987, the Ministère des Finances in 1989, the Parc de Bercy in 1994 and various new residential districts. Below the Jardin des Plantes the boulevards lead to the Place d'Italie and, toward the Porte de Choisy, to the towers of Chinatown (1970), erected at the foot of the Butte-aux-Cailles.

ZIRYAB

LE TRAIN BLEU

RESTAURANTS

Le Temps des Cerises (H A4)
→ 18, rue de la Butte-aux-Cailles (13ᵗʰ)
Tel. 01 45 89 69 48
Mon-Sat noon–2pm, 7.30–11.45pm.
Workers' cooperative offering an informal place to eat. Home-cooking with the occasional exotic influence. Generous portions, set 3-course menu at 78F. If it's full, try the nearby *Chez Gladines* (Basque specialties) or *Chez Paul* (a little more expensive).

Phô Ban Cuon 14 (H B4)
→ 129, ave. de Choisy (13ᵗʰ)
Tel. 01 45 83 61 15
Daily 9am–11pm.
On the borders of Chinatown, this is the hangout for *phô* enthusiasts (it is available all day). The Vietnamese noodle soup served here is amongst the best in Paris. Around 70F.

Le Ziryab (H B1)
→ Institut du Monde Arabe 1, rue des Fossés-St-Bernard (5ᵗʰ). Tel. 01 53 10 10 17
Tue-Sun
noon–3pm (restaurant), 3.30-6pm (tearoom).
At the top of the Institut du Monde Arabe, there is a bird's-eye view of Notre

Dame, north to the Bastille and beyond: a magnificent setting in which to savour a quail *pastilla* (110F), a lamb tajine (140F) or maybe just a mint tea made with fresh leaves (20F).

Le Petit Marguery (H A3)
→ 9, bd de Port-Royal (13ᵗʰ)
Tel. 01 43 31 58 59 Tue-Sat noon–2pm, 7.30–10.15pm.
The epitome of the French bistro, run by the adorable Cousin brothers. Bourgeois cuisine and game in season. Generous portions and regional wine. Tradition at its best. Set menu 165F.

Etchegorry (H A4)
→ 41-43, rue Croulebarbe (13ᵗʰ) Tel. 01 44 08 83 51
Mon-Sat noon–2.30pm, 7–10.30pm.
South-west French cuisine, especially influenced by the Basque country. Reasonable prices. Set menu 145F, gastronomic menu (with *foie gras*) 180F.

Le Train Bleu (H D1)
→ Gare de Lyon
20, bd Diderot (12ᵗʰ)
Tel. 01 43 43 09 06
Daily 11.30am–3pm, 7–11pm.
One of a kind: a station restaurant in a listed historic building. Extraordinary décor with

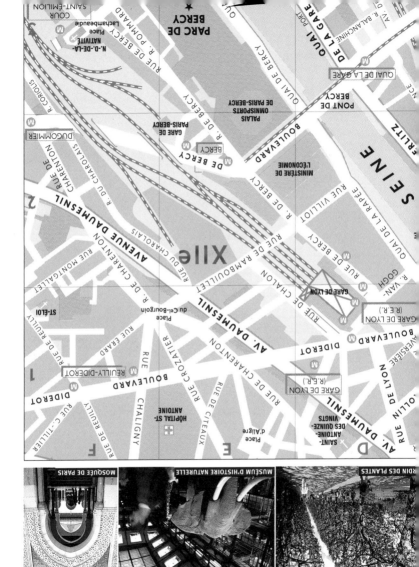

FOLIE EN TÊTE   BERCY VILLAGE   LES ABEILLES

frescos depicting the stops along the Paris-Lyon-Méditerranée (PLM) line, statues, moldings and 1900s furniture. Eager service and good classic cuisine: creamed lentils with bacon and browned croûtons, pike dumplings with crawfish. Set menu 255F.

CAFÉS, TEAROOMS

Bercy Village (H F4)
→ *Cour St-Émilion (12th)*
These former Bercy *chais* (wine cellars) are the perfect place to stop for a drink as they have now been refurbished and turned into café-restaurants.
Salon de Thé de la Mosquée de Paris (H A2)
→ *39, rue Geoffroy-St-Hilaire (5th)*
Tel. 01 43 31 18 14 Daily 8am–11.30pm (tearoom)
Tel. 01 43 31 18 14 (baths)
Women: Mon, Wed-Sat 10am–9pm (Fri 2–9pm)
Men: Tue 2–9pm;
Sun 10am–9pm.
Small tables under the olive and fig trees, the murmur of the fountain, the sweet smell of incense: this setting is straight out of *The Arabian Nights*: Moorish interior and sofas inside

the mosque. Eat a full meal or simply sample the crunchy honey-, almond-, or orange flower-flavored pastries. But before that, why not indulge yourself in the hammam's tempting steam rooms?

BARS, CINEMA, MUSIC VENUES

La Folie en tête (H A4)
→ *33, rue de la Butte-aux-Cailles (13th)*
Tel. 01 45 80 65 99
Mon–Sat 5pm–2am.
A lively little café decorated with wooden musical instruments from all over the world, in the heart of the old village of Butte-aux-Cailles. Contemporary art exhibitions, occasional concerts, storytelling and theater.
Batofar (H E3)
→ *Port de la Gare, opposite 11, quai Mauriac (13th) Tel. 01 56 29 10 00 (times vary depending on the program).*
The latest addition to the trendy fleet of restaurants anchored at the foot of the Bibliothèque Nationale. Steel hull and interior: urban films and exhibitions, electronic music and international

DJs – and a crowd on hand to rock the boat!
Guinguette Pirate (H E3)
→ *Port de la Gare, facing n° 11, quai Mauriac (13th) Tel. 01 56 29 10 20 Daily from 7pm.*
Eclectic clientele and a charged atmosphere in this wooden junk built in Saigon in 1970. Its neighbor, the barge *Makara*, has a different program of music every evening: rock, world music, dub, jazz, reggae, funk, trip hop. Shows for children.
Gaumont Grand Écran Italie (H A4)
→ *30, pl. d'Italie (13th) Tel. 01 45 80 86 78*
Spectacular films shown on the biggest screen in Paris (860 sq ft). Housed in a monochrome, aluminium building designed by Kenzo Tange.

SHOPPING

Galeries d'Art de la rue Louise-Weiss (H C3-C4)
These art galleries now occupy the workshops which once flourished in this former industrial district. They continue the tradition of the great 'Frigos', the former refrigerated warehouses

of Bercy converted into studios which have, since 1980, welcomed into their thousands of square feet at n° 91, quai Panhard-et-Levassor, a plethora of painters, sculptors, architects and musicians.
Les Abeilles (H A4)
→ *21, rue de la Butte-aux-Cailles (13th)*
Tel. 01 45 81 43 48
Tue-Sat 11am–7pm.
Fifty types of honey from all over France.
Mavrommatis (H A2)
→ *47, rue Censier (5th)*
Tel. 01 45 35 96 50
Daily 9am–10pm.
A lovely top-of-the-range Greek deli selling various *meze: talassini*, stuffed vine leaves, aubergine or pepper *caviar* (puréed with a garlic and olive oil marinade). Wide choice of Greek and Cypriot wines.
Marché de la Place Monge (H A2)
→ *Wed, Fri and Sun.*
Attractive little food market close to the Rue Mouffetard.
Tang Frères (H B2)
→ *48, ave. d'Ivry (13th)*
Tel. 01 45 70 80 00
Tue-Sun 9am–7.30pm.
The largest and most famous Asian super-market in the capital, a few steps from Place d'Italie (off the map).

TRAINS & STATIONS

Six stations serve the main regions of France: Gare du Nord (north), Gare de l'Est (northeast), Gare de Lyon (southeast), Gare d'Austerlitz (southwest), Gare Montparnasse (west, southwest), Gare Saint-Lazare (northwest).
TGV: Links Paris to several major cities (Nantes, Lyon) in France and the rest of Europe.
Thalys: Paris–Amsterdam (4¼ hours) via Brussels (1½ hours).
Eurostar: Paris–London (3 hours).
SNCF information
→ Tel. 08 36 35 35 35 35

TAXIS

The white sign 'Taxi' indicates that taxis are free. When they are in use they display a small orange light.
Taxis Bleus
→ Tel. 01 49 36 10 10
Taxis G7
→ Tel. 01 47 39 47 39

CARS

are frescos in the dining room and an outrageous mirror which has pride of place at reception.
Single rooms start at 325F.
Double rooms are light and spacious with 2 large beds, 500F.
Hôtel Gilden Magenta (**C** F1)
→ 35, rue Yves-Toudic (10th) Tel. 01 42 40 17 72
This establishment, tucked away in a quiet little road between République and the Canal Saint-Martin, offers well-equipped rooms from 380F. Pleasant patio where you can eat break-fast; there is also the option of using the kitchen. Reductions for groups of young people (by advance reservation).

400–500F

Hôtel du Globe (**A** C2)
→ 15, rue des Quatre-Vents (6th) Tel. 01 43 26 35 50

Closed Aug.
Gorgeous 17th-century building. The interior decoration is eccentric but appealing. The rooms have floral drapes, exposed beams and stonework, stylish furniture and fresh flowers. From 410F.
Hôtel Esméralda (**A** D2)
→ 4, rue St-Julien-le-Pauvre (5th) Tel. 01 43 54 19 20
In a cobbled street, this 17th-century building giving onto the Square Vivienne houses a 19-room institution. Quirky little hotel with a garden, a view of Notre Dame, exposed stone walls, red velvet sofas, plants, uneven floors and a cat! Book well in advance. From 450–520F.
Hôtel de l'Espérance (**A** E4)
→ 5, rue Pascal (5th) Tel. 01 47 07 10 99
Hotel situated at the bottom of Rue Mouffetard, with 38 lovely rooms, each

different to the next: pastel tones, floral curtains, four-poster beds. Breakfast is served in the small garden in good weather. From 440–550F.
Familia Hôtel (**A** E2)
→ 11, rue des Écoles (5th) Tel. 01 43 54 55 27
The patron is very helpful to guests. Exposed beams or stonework, balconies with flowers, old-fashioned furniture and carpets, frescos of Paris, and a view of Notre Dame. From 460F. Just next door, the brand new Hôtel Minerve, owned by the same proprietor, offers the same service.
Hôtel des Croisés (**E** B5)
→ 63, rue Saint-Lazare (9th) Tel. 01 48 74 78 24
Superb retro-style reception (wrought-iron elevator, red carpets) and period-style rooms from 470F. Double rooms (500F) are very spacious, fitted out with Art-Deco style

Documentation
You may be required to show your insurance, vehicle registration documents and your driving license.
Speed limits
50 kmph (30 mph) in town.
Parking
(10F per hour) Mon-Fri, and Sat depending on the area. Purchase tickets from parking ticket machines, using the correct change. Free parking on Sun and public holidays and in some areas on Sat and during August.
Car pounds
Badly parked cars will be towed away to a car pound. To retrieve your vehicle, contact the nearest police station or the police headquarters:
→ Tel. 01 53 71 53 53

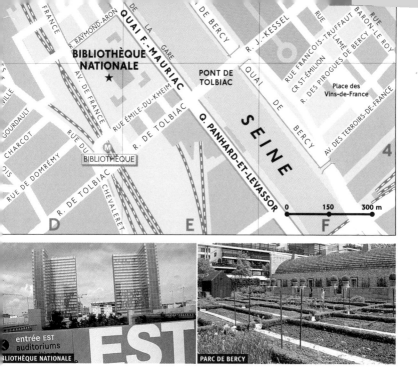

entrée EST
auditoriums
BIBLIOTHÈQUE NATIONALE

PARC DE BERCY

e public. It was taken
er by the Natural History
useum in 1793.

Mosquée de Paris (**H** A2)
1, pl. du Puits-de-l'Ermite
) Tel. 01 43 31 18 14
sed Fri.
is temple to the Muslim
igion was the first to be
ilt in Paris (1922-6). It
s a rich Mediterranean
fluence and is a feast
the eyes: mosaics,
darwood carvings and
finest lattice work –
ch interior created by
al craftsmen. The fairy-
e mosque is arranged
und a courtyard and
oor gardens and has a
mmam, a salon de thé,

restaurant and stores at
nⁿ[os] 39-41, rue Geoffroy-St-
Hilaire.

★ **Chapelle St-Louis-de-
la-Salpêtrière** (**H** C2)
→ 47, bd de l'Hôpital (13ᵗʰ)
Daily 8.30am–6.30pm.
Located within the walls
of one of Paris' oldest
hospitals and built at the
request of Louis XIV, this
chapel (1677) is in the form
of a Greek cross topped
with an astonishing
octogonal dome. It now
provides a setting for
concerts and exhibitions.

★ **Manufacture des
Gobelins** (**H** A3)
→ 42, rue des Gobelins (5ᵗʰ)
Tel. 01 44 08 52 00

Tue-Thu at 2pm and 2.45pm
This royal tapestry work-
shop, founded in 1601 by
Henry IV, was appointed
furniture-maker to the
Crown in 1667. It also
contains 17th- and 18th-
century tapestries
designed by Van der
Meulen and beautiful
religious gold artefacts.

★ **Bibliothèque
Nationale de France**
(**H** D4)
→ quai François-Mauriac
(13ᵗʰ) Tel. 01 53 79 59 59
Tue-Sat 10am–8pm; Sun
noon–7pm (reception, east
visitors hall). www.bnf.fr
The four book-shaped
towers of the 'Très Grande

Bibliothèque' were devised
by Dominique Perrault.
They hold some 10 million
works which cover more
than 260 miles of shelving.
There are advanced
reference systems and
the latest in conservation
techniques. The reading
rooms are arranged around
a delightful indoor garden.
Temporary exhibitions.

★ **Parc de Bercy** (**H** E3)
→ quai de Bercy (12ᵗʰ) Daily.
In 1994 the wine store-
houses of Bercy gave way
to the development of a
33-acre park: botanical
gardens, lawns, an orchard,
a kitchen garden and a
romantic-style garden.

Roissy
Charles-
de-Gaulle
30 km

PARIS

15 km

Orly

N
↑

AIRPORTS

Flight information
→ Tel. 08 36 68 15 15
→ www. adp.fr
General information
Roissy Charles-
de-Gaulle (CDG)
→ Tel. 01 48 62 22 80
Orly
→ Tel. 01 49 75 52 52

PARIS AIRPORTS LINKS

Paris to Roissy CDG
RER B
→ Direct to CDG2 and
courtesy bus to CDG 1.
Roissybus
→ Rue Scribe, M° Opéra
Price 48F.
Air France shuttle
→ Porte Maillot, Étoile,
Montparnasse. Price 60F.
Paris to Orly
Orlyval
→ RER B to Antony, then
Orlyval. Price 57F.
Orlybus
→ In front of RER Denfert-
Rochereau. Price 35F.
Air France shuttle
→ M° Montparnasse
Invalides. Price 45F.

AIRPORT

Except otherwise stated, the prices given are for a double room with en-suite bathroom. In peak season, make reservations at least a month in advance.

YOUTH HOSTELS

Price per person. Single or double rooms and accommodation in dormitories.
Résidence Bastille (F C3)
→ 151, ave. Ledru-Rollin, (11ᵗʰ) Tel. 01 43 79 53 86
Modern building with 150 beds. From 125–175F for a single room (including breakfast).
Hotels M. I. J. E. (C E4)
→ 6, rue de Fourcy (4ᵗʰ) Tel. 01 42 74 23 45
Right in the middle of the Marais, two 17th-century buildings and a medieval house have been converted into this youth hostel. Exceptional setting, comfortable and

relaxed atmosphere. 160F for the dormitories (reserved for 18–30 year-olds), 185F for a double room, breakfast included. Set dinner for 60F.

UNDER 250F

Hôtel Vicq d'Azir (G A4)
→ 21, rue Vicq d'Azir (10ᵗʰ) Tel. 01 42 08 06 70
Close to the Canal Saint-Martin, 70 very modest rooms, some with a view over a verdant little courtyard. From 117F (197F with shower).
Hôtel Henri-IV (A D1)
→ 25, pl. Dauphine (1ˢᵗ) Tel. 01 43 54 44 53
Fabulous location on the very chic Place Dauphine. True, this 16th-century hotel is rather spartan, if not run down, but the rooms have views onto the prettiest square in Paris. From 215F (280F with shower). Book in advance.

Hôtel du Palais (C C3)
→ 2, quai de la Mégisserie (1ˢᵗ) Tel. 01 42 36 98 25
Currently undergoing restoration work. The rooms which have already been renovated are much brighter and offer a view over the Île de la Cité. Ask for a room with double glazing. From 36F (shower and WC on the same floor).

250–400F

Hôtel Sainte-Marie (C C1)
→ 6, rue de la Ville-Neuve (2ᵗʰ) Tel. 01 42 33 21 61
Close to the Grands Boulevards. Attractive, quiet rooms from 250F (340F with bathroom). Friendly reception.
Hôtel du Séjour (C D2)
→ 36, rue du Grenier-Saint-Lazare (3ʳᵈ) Tel. 01 48 87 40 36
Near the Pompidou center

in the Halles area, this hotel offers modest, but recently redecorated rooms. Small interior courtyard. From 280F.
Hôtel Eiffel Rive Gauche (E C4)
→ 6, rue du Gros-Caillou (7ᵗʰ) Tel. 01 45 51 24 56
Four floors built around a small patio. The somewhat scruffy rooms are gradually being done up in a Provençal style. Two small double rooms (305F no shower) have a view of the Eiffel tower; from 445F with shower.
Hôtel Jeanne d'Arc (C E3)
→ 3, rue de Jarente (4ᵗʰ) Tel. 01 48 87 62 11
This 17th-century hotel is on the corner of a quiet, pretty street in the Marais. It has been decorated with the works of artists who are regulars to the hotel... they may not be to everybody's taste. There

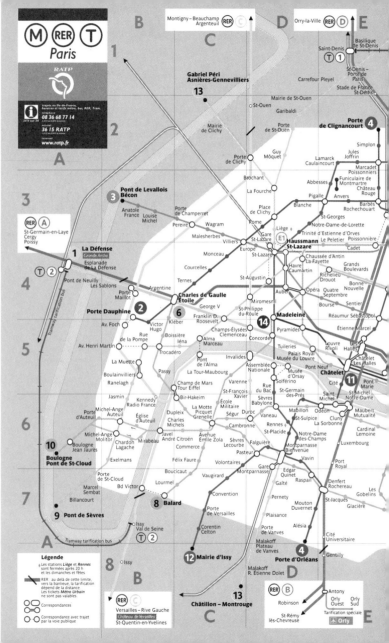

Public transport and hotels in Paris

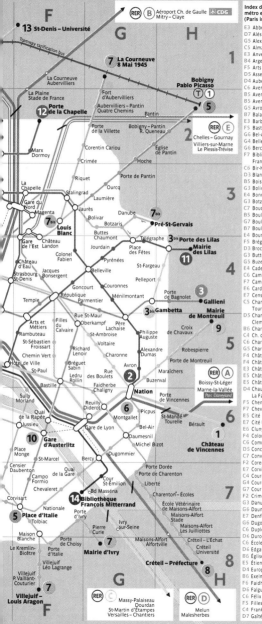

THE NEWLY OPENED LINE 14: MÉTÉOR

reception all contribute to the charm of the place. Rooms from 680F with a rooftop view of Paris and the Sacré Cœur. Breakfast is served in what used to be the dressing rooms of 'Dom Juan', a former 1930s cabaret.

Hôtel des Grands Hommes (A D3)
→ pl. du Panthéon (5th)
Tel. 01 46 34 19 60
This elegant 18th-century hotel has 32 spacious rooms with exposed beams and wrought-iron bedheads. Views of the Pantheon dome from the 6th-floor balconies. Reserve well in adavance. From 750F.

OVER 800F

Hôtel des Jardins du Luxembourg (A C3)
→ 5, Impasse Royer-Collar (5th) Tel. 01 40 60 08 88
In 1883 Freud stayed here.

This splendid hotel has now been completely renovated in a Provençal style: kilims, wood-paneling, small balconies, flowers and tiling give the rooms an unforgettable charm. The extremely spacious Room 1 even has its own entrance. Sauna, elevator, patio and air-conditioning. From 810F.

Hôtel des Marronniers (A B1)
→ 21, rue Jacob (6th)
Tel. 01 43 25 30 60
A good address. Views of the clocktower of Saint-Germain or the garden from some of the rooms. Breakfast is served on the veranda. From 825F.

PALACES

Hôtel Raphaël (D A1)
→ 17, ave Kléber (16th)
Tel. 01 53 64 32 00
www.raphael-hotel.com
A minute's walk from the

Champs-Élysées, this is probably the smallest but most charming of Parisian palaces. Ninety rooms and suites whose antique furniture is cared for daily by the in-house cabinet-maker. Aubusson tapestries, 18th-century inspired mural paintings, Louis-XV wood paneling, and magnificent views of the Arc de Triomphe from the 7th floor. There, on the biggest and most romantic terrace in Paris, have lunch or just a drink. From 2,700F.
And if a night at the Ritz (tel. 01 43 16 30 30), the Crillon (tel. 01 44 71 15 00), the Plaza-Athénée (tel. 01 53 67 66 65) or the Hôtel Costes (tel. 01 42 44 50 00) is just a dream, why not treat yourself to breakfast there (expect to pay between 200 and 350F). Smart dress required. Book in advance.

urniture, marble fireplaces nd with a view of Sacré œur.

00–600F

Résidence hôtelière e Vert Galant (H A4)
→ 41–43, rue Croulebarbe 3th) Tel. 01 44 08 83 50
ifteen stunning, recently enovated rooms, from ooF. This residential hotel lso offers 5 studios vith kitchenettes. Garden nd lawns.

Hôtel Saint-Charles
→ 6, rue de l'Espérance 3th) Tel. 01 45 89 56 54
ight in the heart of utte-aux-Cailles, a light nd airy hotel overlooking pretty interior garden. Vell-equipped rooms, ome a little tatty, are i the process of being edecorated.
rom 498F–720F.

Hôtel du Cygne (C C2)
→ 3, rue du Cygne (1st)

Tel. 01 42 60 14 16
In a pedestrianized street in the Halles quartier. The rooms are small but fully equipped. The hotel has a pleasant décor with exposed beams and a Provençal feel. From 510F. Attractive small courtyard with a veranda where you can sit in comfort and eat breakfast.

Hôtel Agora (C C2)
→ 7, rue de la Cossonnerie (1st) Tel. 01 42 33 46 02
A quiet, well-situated establishment with comfortable, light rooms. View of the church of Sainte-Eustache from the upper floors.
From 540F–730F.

Hôtel des Grandes-Écoles (A E3)
→ 75, rue du Cardinal-Lemoine (5th) Tel. 01 43 26 79 23
A villa resembling a country manor with a private garden in the middle of Paris and just a few yards

from the Contrescarpe (city walls)! Complete peace and quiet, and a large terrace for sunbathing. The décor of this late 19th-century bourgeois house is immaculate: floral wallpaper, antique furniture. Fifty large rooms from 550F.

600–800F

Hôtel du Vieux Saule (C E2)
→ 6, rue de Picardie (3rd) Tel. 01 42 72 01 14
A beautiful hotel, easily identifiable from its flower-covered façade. Comfortable, modern rooms from 590F (complete with air conditioning and free sauna). Breakfast is served in the vault. Small garden and exhibition of antiques in the prudly displayed 'high-tech' lobby.

Hôtel Saint-Louis-du-Marais (C E4)
→ 1, rue Charles-V (4th)

Tel. 01 48 87 87 04
Closed Aug.
A tiny residence, renovated and furnished in a traditional style. Rooms from 685–785F. Exposed beams and vault.

Hôtel Bersoly's Saint-Germain (B D4)
→ 28, rue de Lille (7th) Tel. 01 42 60 73 79
Closed Aug.
A 17th-century townhouse with a hushed atmosphere. Small rooms with exposed beams and period furniture, each dedicated to a different painter and decorated with reproductions of the artist's work. From 662–762F.

Hôtel Royal Fromentin (E B4)
→ 11, rue Fromentin (9th) Tel. 01 48 74 85 93
This address is highly prized among musicians. The wood paneling, the windows, the wrought-iron elevator and the friendly

Letters (**A, B, C...**) relate to the matching sections. Letters on their own refer to the useful addresses spreads and, where followed by a star (**A★**), to the places of interest on the fold-out map of the area.